Dear Jane.

With very happy memories.

Good luck with your music.

Love Joan

7th May 81.

Patterns of Australia

by Geoffrey Dutton **Patterns**

# of Australia

Photographs by Harri Peccinotti

Published by The Macmillan Company of Australia Pty Ltd., in association with Mobil Oil Australia Ltd.

For Nin, companion of all my journeys.

'The writer's aim does not consist in resolving the questions posed, but in instilling a love of life in all its innumerable and inexhaustible manifestations.'

Leo Tolstoy

Text © Geoffrey Dutton
Photographs by Harri Peccinotti
Editor: Gregory Vitiello
Art director & designer: Derek Birdsall
Production: Martin Lee
Printed in Australia by Griffin Press Limited
Typesetting and origination by Balding & Mansell

Published by Macmillan Company of Australia Pty Ltd.,
in association with Mobil Oil Australia Ltd.

Foreword

More than once, I have wished for a book that presented Australia to the world – and to Australians – in its variety, its complexity and its beauty. Many books, of course, do one job or the other: some contain excellent photographs but oversimplify the character of Australia; other fine books such as Manning Clark's *History of Australia* and Geoffrey Blainey's *Triumph of the Nomads* explain the country without showing it.

For me the lack of a handsome, intellectually rich book was most pronounced when I went to Peking some years ago as a guest of the Chinese government. During my visit I was given every opportunity to study the people and culture of China, and to gain new insights into this ancient land. I, for my part, wanted to return the favour in some small measure: to give my hosts a book which presented my country to them in a similarly memorable way.

The lack of such a book prompted Mobil to commission Geoffrey Dutton to write *Patterns of Australia*. What we asked of him was demanding: a book which explores the events and influences that have shaped Australia and Australians. We did not ask him to shy away from controversy; as a result, there are opinions in the book with which many people may not agree. What is important is that they are Geoffrey Dutton's opinions: always intelligent, often provocative, informed with a passion for things Australian. The photographs, by Harri Peccinotti, are personal – and, I think, extraordinary. They are the work of a man who brought a fresh eye and rare aesthetic quality to his job.

I hope *Patterns of Australia* will contribute to the growing appreciation of those things which make our country unique.

Jim Leslie
Chairman, Mobil Oil Australia Ltd.
1980

Preface

In the thick shade of mango trees by the Pacific Ocean north of Cairns, I discussed with Greg Vitiello and Jim Cass from Mobil their company's idea for a book about Australia. 'Imagine', suggested Greg, 'half a dozen friends sitting around having a drink, talking about Australia. A couple of them are Australians, and the others have never been there. "But what's Australia really like?" one of them asks. "What moulded and shaped it to be what it is today?" asks another.'

This is my attempt to answer such questions. Of course the subject is vast; it would be impossible even to begin to cover it in one short book. Nor have I tried to write a factual or explanatory book; there are some excellent factual books already available, such as Craig McGregor's, and several brilliant analyses by Donald Horne.

I have tried instead to interpret various aspects of Australia and Australians through my own lifetime experience of them, modified by many years of travel abroad, and also to illuminate this study by reference to Australia's history and culture, especially literature and art. There are many areas of Australian life and Australian passions that I have not mentioned, such as gambling or football, partly because the sports I like are different ones, such as fishing and swimming, and partly because, although millions of Australians are crazy about football, so are even more millions of Germans, Russians and Argentinians. (Although Australian Rules fanatics would rise up in wrath saying, '*Our* football is *different*.')

The book has three themes, sometimes brought out into the open, sometimes left hidden to make their own way. The first is that no one who has experienced Australia through the last 20 years can doubt that this period has been the most exciting and full of change in all Australian history, even more than the legendary 1890's. Instead of spelling out the changes, I have introduced them, by anecdote and comparison, into all the chapters of the book. The second is that Australians, especially those who run affairs or are listened to and read in the media, are woefully under-confident about their own country and people. Needless to say, I am not advocating a grating nationalism, 'Australia's the best bloody country in the world, mate, and if you don't agree with me I'll knock your teeth down the back of your neck.' That sort of Ockerism is irrelevant.

Australia is groping towards a true understanding of itself as a nation after the '50's to '70's expansion which has left it in a state of shock, not understood by those living through it. Australia is so different in so many ways from what it was 20 years ago, and yet so unmistakably Australian still, that it is no wonder that it is hard to resolve the old and the new. Yet the capacity of acceptance in ordinary people is always astonishing in its quality. This can be illustrated by taking a walk down Rundle Mall, in Adelaide, in my home State of South Australia. Twenty years ago Rundle Street, Adelaide's shopping centre, was a narrow and noisome street jammed with traffic, cars parked on both sides, buses ploughing through, with air more polluted than anything in London or New York. Now, closed to traffic and called Rundle Mall, it is paved with brown bricks, there are trees and open-air cafes and buskers singing and playing guitars and recorders. People sit and look, walk as they please, flirt and laugh. Already the people have accepted it all. And if life can look so different, then people must feel different, be less prepared to put up with the worst, happier to accept the best.

Rundle Mall is only a token. There are hundreds more. Australians for so long have been resigned to looking for excellence somewhere else, or as something imported; now these standards are being achieved in Australia.

My third theme is that the Australian countryside, whether close to the cities, in the Outback, or in the North, because of its very nature and because of being so sparsely populated, has a unique power to heal.

This power was felt immediately by Harri Peccinotti and his assistant Geneviève Hamelet who had come, on their first visit to Australia, to work on the photographs for this book. My wife and I took them out on a houseboat on the river Murray, and then camping to the far north of the Flinders Ranges of South Australia, and it was a joy to see their response. Harri and Geneviève spent six weeks travelling all over Australia, and Harri's thousands of photographs were so good that it was extremely difficult to make the selection used in this book. I have the happiest memories of long hours spent in London at the Covent Garden studio of the book's designer, Derek Birdsall, going through the photographs again and again with Gregory Vitiello, Harri and Geneviève, and sumptuously sustained by the good Yorkshire cooking of Derek's wife Shirley. One of the most pleasant things about writing this book has been the good fellowship of working with such people, and with Jim Cass and Pamela Oddy in Melbourne.

I would like to thank Jim Leslie, Robin Marrett and Mobil Oil Australia Ltd, without whose impetus and help the book could not have been written, and also the manager in Western Australia, Fred Forgan, and agents along the tracks from Carnarvon to Darwin, for all their help and information.

Geoffrey Dutton

Loving and hating Australia

To get to know Australia you still have to explore it, just as those who made the first landfall, took in the first inland distances, touched the first stones or rolled a dry leaf in the hand and breathed in the aromatic essence of its brown fragments. The language and rituals of the inhabitants can be tackled later.

This is especially true of Australia, for it is so different from any other country. Nostalgic Australians abroad may sometimes catch a glimpse of it, in the cleansing light of Greece, in the dust and spiky bushes of Natal, the Sudan or Morocco, or in a eucalyptus avenue in California. But the true aromatic essence is only to be found at home, whether dry and crackling from drought, or secret and soft under the tree ferns of the coastal rain forests.

Although Australia is the most urbanized of the world's large countries, with its nine or 10 biggest cities all around the coast, and although the big money no longer comes from wool, meat or wheat, the country itself, the bush and the outback, still guards and sometimes threatens Australian life. At times there are warnings that even city people with their pavement-focused eyes cannot ignore, when there is no vegetation to hold down the droughty topsoil and the wind blows it in red dust for a thousand miles, 10,000 feet high, and when a thunderstorm hits the city the car windscreen wipers have to shove their way through red mud. When the season breaks after three years of drought a greening of hope ripples over the concrete and asphalt. The taxi driver says to you, *There's a sort of a lift everywhere, you can see it in people. I come from the Mallee myself*, he adds, *those poor buggers deserved a break*.

The Mallee, that lean five- to 15-inch rainfall country, stretches on and off for nearly 2,000 miles from Western Australia across South Australia to Victoria and New South Wales. The tree itself, after which the Mallee is called, forms a characteristic family among the 500 eucalypts, and fans out from the knobbly drought-resistant root, its trunk different colours at different times, its blossoms cascading with budgerigars.

After almost 200 years, Australians are at last learning to love their country for what it is, for the relish of uniqueness that goes beyond the comfort of similarity. For many years people who

Victorian bluestone, Melbourne jail.

would unhesitatingly identify themselves as Australians also gave their deepest loyalties to Britain, not only fighting her wars, standing up for her Queen or King, flying her flag, singing her anthem, but also actually calling Britain 'Home'. Millions of Australians talked about 'going Home' when they meant taking a boat to London. Moreover, they surrounded themselves with trees and flowers, books, pictures, magazines that were not Australian. It was as if there was some separate race called 'British', still part of a mystical British Empire even when the reality had collapsed, ready to burst into tears at a singing of *Land of Hope and Glory*.

Those who crossed the Atlantic from Europe to America at least found vegetation that was familiar; Australia did not offer even that comfort. The native people, the Aborigines, were much more remote, more withdrawn into the past than the Indians. The Aborigines understood Australia as the whites did not begin to for many years; they knew how to live off it, to crack its seeds with fire, but their beliefs were so different that most white people thought they had 'no religion'. Their religion was in fact Australia, going back to the dreamtime, and their beliefs animated the rocks and waterholes and made them sacred. But to the white Australians the past that was sacred was the past of other countries, enshrined in the Palestine of Jesus, preserved more intimately in the lush meadows and accessible ruins of Britain.

For these British Australians, Australia could only be a perpetual disappointment, even at times a harsh, awkward, ungenerous surface to be hated. Everything had to be brought. The Aborigines had no crops, no herds. There were fish in the sea and the rivers, and ducks on both. But the meat of kangaroos, emus, cockatoos or snakes was a diet of desperation. Then, too soon, all the imports went berserk. There were rabbits, foxes, sparrows, oxalis (soursob), viper's bugloss (Salvation Jane in South Australia, Paterson's Curse in New South Wales) and cactus. It was ironic that this drought-stricken country that had to be coaxed into growing wheat, and watered carefully to produce a peach or a geranium, should on its own, without any help from man beyond the initial importation, pour out an insane excess of pests. It was the ultimate cruelty that in times of drought the sheep- and cattlemen of the interior should see the fruitless mulga that offers stock its low-hanging boughs, bulging with starving rabbits, climbing the furthest branches to eat the bark and kill the tree.

Millions of British Australians hated the grimy pores of their new country, which could never have the soft skin of England's green and pleasant land. People whose vision was trained by the village and hedge, church spire and thatched cottage, could literally not believe their eyes when they had to take in Australia's distances.

In practical terms, distance in Australia was, and is, an enemy to be overcome. And even that which is close is not always friendly. The ecology of Australia mocks the accepted canons of the aesthetic and the romantic. Stop to look at the stamens of a flowering gum, and a moment later you find you are standing on a bullant's nest. Walk closer to stroke the taut female sleekness of its bark, and the ants are scurrying up to the blossom, while if you peel a loose brown piece of bark away there is a black spider underneath it. If you walk longingly towards the broken blue of the far ranges, you are enveloped in flies. Lovers, looking for a secluded spot behind the tea tree's close screen, should first make sure there is no snake by the log, no centipede under the bough. There is also a certain spider that drops a thousand of its babies upon those who lie under the tea tree.

Australia makes nothing easy, except for its marvellous beaches, which may be one reason why Australians, though not a seafaring people, are a seashore-going one. The beach is also an area where those people who do not chase balls or drive beach-buggies are forced to go slow and be still, except when they are wrestling with the surf.

There is something sexual in the relation of people to their country. People talk of loving or hating it, or of its being ravished or raped. In such terms, Australia is not an easy, romantic conquest, but a creative force, an adversary, who says: *Don't call me by those loving names. Show me you really love me.*

Those who have the deepest relationship with the country

must accept its idiosyncracies and love both its distance and its details. If nothing is given easily, nothing surrounded in a romantic glow, it is all the more passionately to be apprehended. *She's a bastard of a country, but she'll do me*, is in fact a profound declaration of love.

Our trees, shedding their bark rather than their leaves, baffled observers from the earliest artists and settlers, who were offended at their untidiness, down to the poet A.D. Hope, who grumbled at them for wearing the field-grey uniform of modern wars. The Greeks, who populated their woods with dryads, nymphs of the trees, would never have made such a mistake.

Unlike living creatures, whose dry blood is something sad and dead, the gum that trickles down a white or terracotta trunk has a gleaming richness in its filtered light. The inner coolness can only be found by peeling off the curving dead bark, then rubbing away the white powder of the trunk to reveal the skin of the tree, green in midsummer's pale gold. Even on those black-trunked trees, the surly stringybarks and ironbarks, the sparkling gum bleeds out from the scabs of bark, as if each tree had survived a separate bushfire. And out on the edges of the desert there is the mulga, with its shellac-curly bark glowing transparent red, host to a thousand ants.

The relationship between the seemingly implacable surface of Australia and its extraordinary beauty is symbolic of the difficulty in establishing an emotional relationship to both the distance and the closeness of Australia. As the historian Geoffrey Blainey explained in his book *The Tyranny of Distance*, the nation was moulded by its distance from the rest of the world and the distance enfolded in its own interior vastness. The same old statistics can never be produced often enough: while Australia is more or less the same size as the United States of America, its population is about 14 million, far less than a tenth of that of the USA. The traveller flying from New York to San Francisco sees a variety of richness, and one great city after another goes under the wing. But the traveller from Sydney to Perth sees one city, Adelaide, and a few country towns; the good cropping and grazing country gives way to the Mallee, sand in parallel waves beginning to drift where

the Mallee has been cleared and the crops have failed, and then in the centre there is the Nullarbor plain, with no trees and vast hidden limestone caves, where no water can be caught and held on the surface, even when the tiny rainfall comes down.

Terra Australis Incognita, the unknown southern land, was thought to stretch right to the south pole. Whether the earth was believed to be flat or round, this southern emptiness was always at the bottom. Civilization, which was Europe, was at the top. It took a long time before people realized that civilization had come from the middle, from Asia, and even longer before *australis* (southern) became Australia, a separate country where people might live, connected with the rest of the world.

It was the Dutch, not the British, who 'discovered' Australia, and they thought it too desolate and barren to be worth settling. Although the Portuguese and Spaniards were zigzagging through the reefs of New Guinea in the 16th and early 17th centuries, it was Jansz in the *Duyfken* (the name, Little Dove, is haunting, something out of the Ark) who first landed in Australia in 1606 on the coast of the Gulf of Carpentaria, in what is now northern Queensland. In the next 10 years other Dutchmen sailed down the coast of Western Australia, finding none of the precious metals and spices they were hoping for. Carstenz, in 1623, along the west coast of Cape York, wrote gloomily in his journal: *We have not seen one fruit-bearing tree, nor anything that man could make use of . . . It is the most arid and barren region that could be found anywhere on the earth; the inhabitants, too, are the most wretched and poorest creatures that I have seen.* He had in fact been looking at mysteries he did not or could not understand: immense riches of bauxite, for instance, and the life of the Aborigines, which was poor by his standards but not at all wretched.

Only four years later, on the opposite side of the continent, Thijssen and Nuijts sailed for 1,000 miles along the terrible cliffs and giant sandhills of the Great Australian Bight. The extremity of their discoveries, now known as Nuyt's Archipelago, was for Jonathan Swift the end of the world, for he wrecked the *Antelope* a little further on, in what is now South Australia, but which for Lemuel Gulliver was the land of Lilliput. As for the Great

Early morning, River Murray.

Salt Lake, Western Australia.

Australian Bight, the French explorer D'Entrecasteaux, 100 years after the Dutchmen, wrote: *It is not surprising that Nuyts has given no details of this barren coast; its aspect is so uniform that the most fruitful imagination could find nothing to say of it.*

The mysteries of Australia were not easily penetrated. The fruitful imaginations of writers and artists have been needed to find much to say of Australia, whether on the Gulf of Carpentaria or beyond the 600-foot cliffs of the Great Australian Bight.

It is an unkind paradox that the American War of Independence caused the colony of New South Wales (later named Australia) to be born in chains. On 26 January 1788 Captain Arthur Phillip (whose father was a German) took possession of the whole of eastern Australia, including Tasmania, in the name of a Hanoverian, George III. A year later George Washington became the first president of the United States. The colony was a dumping-ground for the convicts who could no longer be sent to America; in the King's speech of January 1787, New Holland, which was to become Australia, was simply an outlet *to remove the inconvenience which arose from the crowded state of the gaols in different parts of the Kingdom.* The first white population of Australia consisted of 736 convicts, 17 children of convicts, 257 marines, wives and children, and 20 officials. Spread across the continent were perhaps 300,000 Aborigines. Beyond the barrier of the Blue Mountains were the plains of the flattest continent on earth, and the white men were to find, after the heartbreaking journeys of the great explorers, that nearly half of the country had a rainfall of less than 10 inches per year.

Settled by convicts, starved by nature of rain and rivers, inhabited by so-called 'savages' who did not relish their land being stolen from them, offering no comforts of history or tradition, Australia was not a place to love. Even the free colony of South Australia, settled in 1836, could offer no more than 18 per cent of non-arid country in the whole state to go with its moral benefits. It is no wonder that even among those who tried to love the country, few could understand it and truly think of its uniqueness as home.

The men who cut the trees and stone of Australia's first roads and buildings wore leg irons of 15 pounds and their backs sustained up to 1,000 lashes from the cat o' nine tails. Yet the British, French and Germans who explored the country by sea and land were free men of culture and education, often admirable writers and talented artists, eccentrics with no prospect of just reward let alone of gain, or simply officers doing their duty. They suffered appalling hardships and yet went back for more. Many of them were also amazingly young, not to be confused with the patriarchs who represent them in official portraits and statues. Flinders was only 21 when he sailed down the New South Wales coast with Bass. Eyre was only 25 and already an experienced explorer when he set off to cross the Nullarbor Plain. Leichhardt had spent years wandering in Europe but was still only 31 when he took his first expedition to the Gulf of Carpentaria. The great Cook himself was only a Lieutenant of 41 when he hoisted the British flag on New South Wales.

Whatever Australia made them suffer, its explorers brought to it a youthful energy, a boundless curiosity and a sense of homage. Australia was totally lacking in white civilization, but all the explorers approached it with the full solemnity and honour of European art and science. The English and French expeditions carried artists and naturalists. (In Cook's case, there were two Germans.) Their magnificent paintings and drawings of the Aborigines, the flora and the fauna are still just beginning to reach the Australian public. The originals were (and are) locked in museums or, if engraved and published, turned over occasionally in gentlemen's libraries. The journals of the explorers, Australia's first authentic literature, had until recently no wide exposure in Australia or anywhere else. Edward John Eyre's magnificent 365 pages on the *Manners and Customs of the Aborigines* still remain tucked away at the back of his journals, scarcely acknowledged even by the experts.

So Australians have grown up with an extraordinary division in their consciousness. Science and art had embraced Australia and formed a culture based on an understanding of the continent's uniqueness. But until the 1930's, maybe even later, Australians were hardly taught any Australian history or literature at school.

People preferred to plant exotic rather than Australian flowers in their gardens; indeed, some of them hardly knew that Australian flowers existed.

The tragedy of the Burke and Wills transcontinental expedition of 1860–1 embodies the failure of Australians, especially those comfortable in the pomposities of Victorian colonial city life, to understand the environment of their adopted country. (Burke was born in Ireland, Wills in England.) Cooper's Creek, where they died, abounds in fish and bird and animal life in a good season such as they had. More than a century after Burke and Wills, nature is still generous. The tumbling white corellas, smaller cousins of the big sulphur-crested cockatoos, saw across the silence of the brown waterholes. The huge brolgas, most elegant of land birds, run lungingly forward to take off from the ankle-deep clover. A good season carpets the earth with blue harebells, cranesbill and billy buttons, yellow everlasting daisies, pink mallows, and the red dots that lift and blow away are tiny red-breasted finches. There are birds to shoot for food, and Burke and Wills had guns and ammunition. Their fishhooks were the wrong size but the friendly Aborigines came and offered them baskets of fish, which Burke repulsed, not wanting to fraternize. King, the only survivor, lived with the Aborigines and had a child by one of their women. Before leaving Melbourne, if Burke had read Eyre on the manners and customs of the blacks he and Wills would also have survived. If they had been bushmen, sympathetic to the blacks like Howitt, who led the search party that found King, they would have survived.

In short, even in 1860 one did not have to have been born in Australia to understand it, to love its peculiarities and not be angered by its lack of familiar comforts, not to mention its inconveniences, the dust and burrs and flies. But the pattern of Burke and Wills was to continue for another century. Grand schemes for the outback hatched in city offices and clubs, like the huge caravan of equipment sent off with Burke and Wills, invariably came to grief. For Australia, like some endless python, quietly swallows them.

The snake, in many tribal areas of Australia, is related to the Rainbow Serpent, the maker of rivers and underground water; he is closely involved with Kunapipi, the Creative Mother herself. By knowing their demands and venerating them, the blacks were also able to live in harmony with Australia as the whites have rarely succeeded in doing.

The whites' culture, plants and animals are all imported, but Australia is large enough to absorb the new and the old. On those terms, as in life, it is possible to reconcile love and hate and live with them without bitterness. In a successful Australian garden there is no conflict between the indigenous gumtree and the imported oak, as long as the climate and soil are respected and both trees are given the water they need.

Western Australia, Indian Ocean.

Fallow paddock blowing away, South Australian Mallee.

Earth, Air, Fire, Water

When Chaucer or Shakespeare talked about the four elements his audience knew he meant earth, air, fire and water. Now there are over a hundred elements and you have to be a scientist to know all of them.

But Australia still has an old-fashioned simplicity, it is elemental, being so empty and so old. Even viewed from the cities this is true. The old earth, with its flowers and trees, is at the back door of all the cities, and sometimes, as in Perth's King's Park or Sydney's Ku-ring-gai Chase, right in the living-room. It is impossible to travel between the cities without being intensely aware of how the earth's shapes and shifts override the squares of fencing or ploughing. From the air the predominant red of Australia shows through all too clearly and all too often; it shows through droughty sparse crops or drifting sandhills, in the hoof trails of cattle or sheep, while the water shrinks in the bare arms of the dam-banks.

Drought is the Australian norm, whether the soil is red loam or sand, the black-soil plains of western New South Wales, the scurfy grey of Canberra and the Monaro, even the black-soil valleys of the Darling Downs. The arid and semi-arid regions, which make up 63 per cent of Australia, don't get much rain, but when it does come, even in the deserts, whole Switzerlands of wildflowers appear miraculously as if in gratitude.

These wildflowers are Australia's subtlest and most characteristic offering from the earth. There is no natural abundance of fruits and nuts; although the Aborigines knew which berries and nuts and roots to eat, the white man has never made anything of them, at best regarding them as survival rations, with some exceptions such as the delicious macadamia nut. Hawaii grows about six times as many macadamias as Australia (a typical example of Australian under-confidence in its own products), which leads many Americans staunchly to maintain that the nuts are Hawaiian.

The flowers are a different matter, though I was once told by a Frenchman that wattles were introduced into Australia by the French explorers. Australian wildflowers and blossoms are unbelievably abundant for short periods, although many of them are modest, and need to be looked for. The one that pours out most richly in all its soft, golden varieties is the wattle. During its short flowering, it is as if the sun itself were pouring honey in great fluffy globes or long delicate sprays. Though there are often whole hillsides covered in wattle, it makes its clearest statement among the dark trunks and sombre leaves of tall gum trees, punctuating the distance with its brilliant bursts of gold.

But for the wildflowers you have to walk, and stop, and look down, in order to find the candid blue orchids, long-legged, green and brown spider orchids, the red running postman, or the feathery insect-eating plants. In one square yard of scrub on Kangaroo Island, off South Australia, we once counted 28 varieties of wildflowers. A slender, spiky elegance is most characteristic of Australian wildflowers, yet there are also plants that make a great bold presence, like the New South Wales red waratahs and the Western Australian wildflowers.

Australia's wildflowers suffer from their uniqueness, just as many of its treasures seem inadequate to the person who is looking for something else. Very few of the early settlers noticed them, and although the botanists listed them it needed the enthusiasm of Germans like Baron von Mueller and Richard Schomburgk to urge people to grow and cherish the native plants. The novelist Miles Franklin, in her autobiography, gives a perfect picture of the bush held at bay, and of the settlers growing their nostalgic gardens of roses, honeysuckle, sweet-william and lilacs. As she puts it, *Mother's garden was a preserve for emigrants stoutly fenced in from wild Australia.*

The birds suffered the same lack of respect as the flowers. Those that were edible, such as the splendid flashing bronze-wing pigeon or the dainty little topknot pigeon, were shot and eaten in vast quantities, while the highly audible but hardly edible parrot and cockatoo family were resented as terrible thieves of garden fruits and freshly sown paddocks of grain. (Recipe: Bake a cockatoo with a stone; when the stone is tender, the cockatoo is ready to eat.) It could be argued that the most beautiful of bird calls is that of the Australian thrush, just as the most beautiful scent of all flowers may be that of boronia, which appears to be so deceptively modest with its little brown and green bells.

But the characteristically irreverent side of Australia comes out strongly in all the birds that do not sing melodiously like the thrush. The kookaburra has an uncanny knack of letting go his mad laughter just when you are doing something a bit foolish. Oddly enough, the kookaburra's laughter often terrified the early settlers; a sense of humour is not the first thing to come ashore in the emigrant's luggage. The lyre-bird is another humorist, though this seems profane against the beauty of the male's plumage; he is a marvellous mimic, copying everything from other birds to wood-chopping. It is bizarre, deep in the forest, under some of the tallest trees in the world, to hear the noises of a camp when you know there is no camp for miles. You can make the same false human reading in the Queensland rain forests, when the whip bird cracks the air. The cockatoo family, the great sulphur-crested and the pink Major Mitchell, the little white corellas, and the grey and pink galahs, seem to be natural clowns, and are no respecters of the famous 'silence of the bush'. I have seen galahs by the hundreds on a power line, some hanging upside down by one claw, cursing and shouting at each other, and once I even saw one spin around the wire on his beak.

Some of the most entertaining Australian birds are the choughs, which are black with curved beaks, and are often called apostle birds because they go around in groups of a dozen or so. They suddenly arrive in the garden, fluting gently, tidying up the beds, treading circumspectly across the lawn, some bowing respectfully with a gleam of white tail feathers before they dig deep, while others whistle softly. Then they all fly into a tree, with an unmusical squawking; fat, untidy, undignified, companionable, sitting so close together that it seems indecently familiar, they cock a tomato-red eye, forage for fleas with curved bills, then scratch with a claw in the same place. They build huge mud nests which they all share, and it is heartrending when a baby falls out of the nest and the whole commune flaps and flutters and cries around it.

Australian birds can be as solitary as eagles or as abundant as budgerigars. The great wedge-tailed eagle, the biggest eagle in

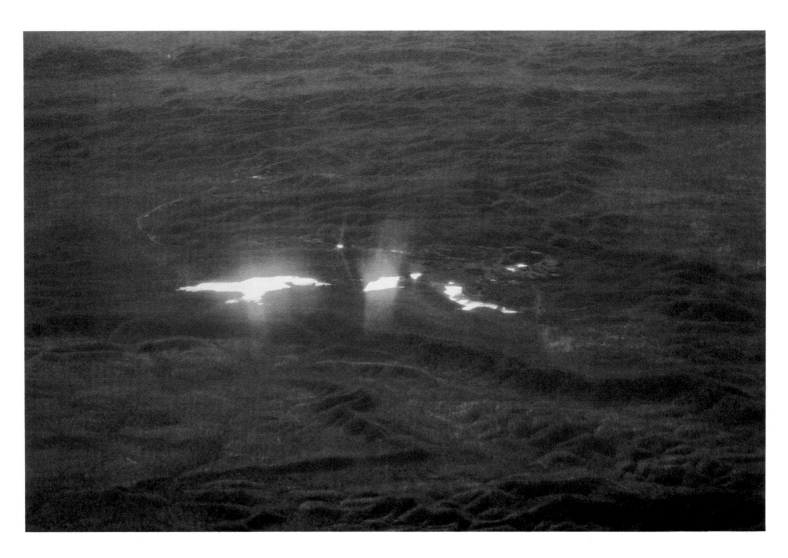

Mining country, Western Australia.

Galahs in grazing country, Western Australia.

the world, with his feathers of black and rusted iron, seems most at home in the distances of the outback, but I have seen him circling peacefully over the freeway through the Adelaide hills, the whole city under his gaze. Best of all is to see him in the paddocks at dawn. Once one took off in front of our car, flying slowly ahead of it. He landed on a fence-post and I stopped the car, no more than a few feet away, and he stayed there staring at us. In the pale early morning he was dark and fierce, with his thick bearded neck, beak strong as an axe, and thick-feathered legs, like no ordinary bird at all, but rather some disturbed guardian of the day.

Budgerigars, on the other hand, can vanish. Out in the Mallee, in a good season when the spear-grass is waist high, I have seen a mob of 800 to 1,000 budgerigars rise in a tight whirring sphere, circle within circle like carved Chinese balls, and then all settle less than 10 yards away in the slender spear-grass and entirely disappear, except for their faint chirring. Then abruptly they will rise and meld with another mob emerging from a desert oak.

Birds are one of the joys of being in the country, but they also come right into the heart of the Australian cities; there are sulphur-crested cockatoos feeding on a Sydney lawn, kookaburras and currawongs taking food from a woman's hand in Canberra, galahs and magpies in an Adelaide park, crimson lowries and spangled drongos (wonderful name!) fighting it out for breakfast in the back garden of a Queensland beach resort. One day in the country, watering my trees from a tank on a trailer behind the tractor, I turned off the engine and listened to the fluting cascades of magpies, and thought that in our dry country we have no sound of running water, no babbling brooks, but instead we have the birds, especially the magpies, streams of song around us all the time.

To hear the sleeping and waking of earth, you need, of course, to live in the country, to move slowly with sheep (or be maddened by them when they rush), to get your hands dirty with dags at crutching, or dodge a bullock in the yards. But this should not be a mystique. Australia, more than any other nation, needs to have its vast majority of city-dwellers regularly exposed to the earth they live on and which keeps them alive.

Chekhov, who had never been to Australia, intuitively knew how Australia *is* the country and the country *is* Australia. In a letter to a friend, he wrote:

It is uncomfortable to live in the country, the season of impassable roads has started, but in nature something amazing, poignant is happening that with its poetry and novelty makes up for all the discomforts of life. Every day there are surprises, one better than the other . . . A day lasts an eternity. You live as in Australia, at the end of the world, your mood is calm, contemplative, animal, in the sense that you don't regret yesterday or wait for tomorrow. From here, from far off, people seem very good, and this is natural, because in retiring to the country we hide not from people but from our vanity, which, in the city, where you are surrounded by people, is unreasonable and inordinate . . .

Not only does the country begin very quickly outside the Australian cities, but country ways of life also take over from the frenetic city pattern. In a city such as Melbourne, Italian market gardeners make a buffer of rows of tomatoes, beans, cauliflowers and glasshouses; their houses are square and bald, for nobody has any time for flowers. They are as separate and justifiable to their own codes as their produce is vital to the community. Their neighbours affect a different style, but just as tightly organized, training greyhounds on a bundle of leashes, or trotters whizzing their little chariots around a dusty circuit.

A hundred miles further on you can find children who have never seen the sea; middle-aged parents who on their rare visits to the city park their car in an outer suburb and take a bus, to avoid the terrors of the traffic; old men who knew what it was like to wear wheatbags instead of a waterproof when ploughing in the rain, back in the hungry '30's. One old man, only 50 miles from a capital city, remembers that on his farm he and his brothers slept in a shed and were only allowed in the house for meals, in case he was tempted to incest by the presence of three sisters.

A farm labourer of 40 says the young people nowadays don't know how hard life can be. Their family of 10 lived in the hills during the Depression. Father hadn't a job but worked for commission on sales for a market gardener. One week he brought home only two shillings and eight pence for the family. They were always barefoot, ragged and usually hungry. When they moved 80 miles into the country it was bitterly cold in the winter and they still never had shoes. A sadistic sportsmaster made them play football in the frost in their bare feet. They had terrible chilblains. They used to walk to school five miles, and if it was raining they shivered all day in school in their wet clothes.

He got his first job, on a farm, earning 10 shillings a week; he started at 3 a.m., milking the cows, and finished late in the afternoon. Often he didn't get his supper till nine. When once, foolishly, he complained of frost-bitten fingers the old farmer called for a bowl of near-boiling water and dipped the boy's fingers in it. Talking about the family who lived nearby, he sounds as if he is talking about a litter of pigs. *Big family, 21 of them, they lost a few, ended up without about 16, I think.* His first really good job was working on the pipeline from the river Murray. He had to ride 12 miles each way on his pushbike. He got £2. 10. 0 a week, and eventually managed to buy his first motor bike. Along with cars, motor bikes were the first allies against Australian distances.

The stories about the people and the land are the closest of kin, from Tasmania to Queensland, from the Pacific to the Indian ocean. The essence of the land, and those who live on it, is that it is local. Each detail – the gate, the trough, the windmill, the rock, the tree – is known and recognizable. Ordinary people only see the road, the fence, the grass, the sky. But country people have dogs' noses; like poets, they discover what is hidden and what gives the visible a new meaning. A city man might see four crows in a tree and drive on, but the countryman stops, goes over and finds a sick ewe under the tree. Countrymen are people who notice, and the earth responds, for it has a bond with them.

They are often wonderfully parochial. In Brisbane a TV reporter who was conducting street interviews on the meaning of Easter stopped a young man, obviously country-bred, and asked him, *What does Easter mean to you?* To which he answered, *I dunno, mate, I dunno what you mean, I come from Bundaberg.* Of course the boy from Bundaberg might have been pulling the TV inter-viewer's leg. Australian country people have a deadly quiet deadpan humour, slow and ironic, that often goes unnoticed and

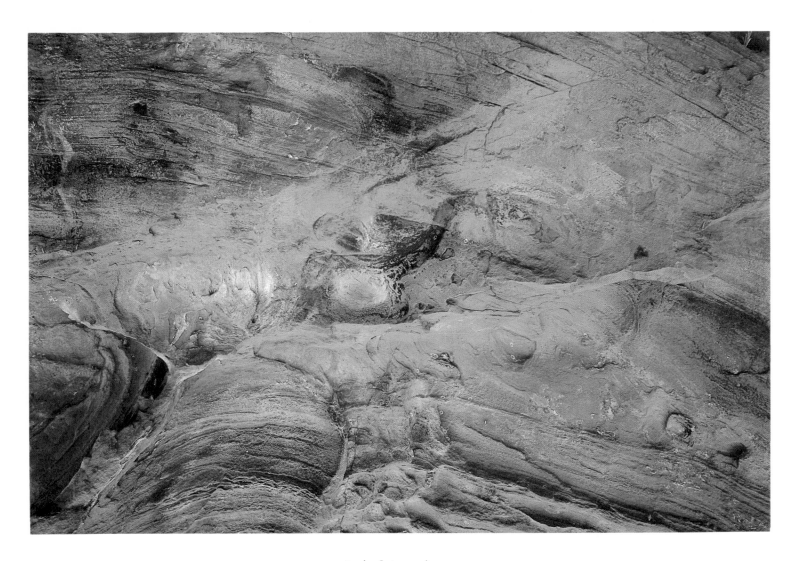

Bark of river red gum.

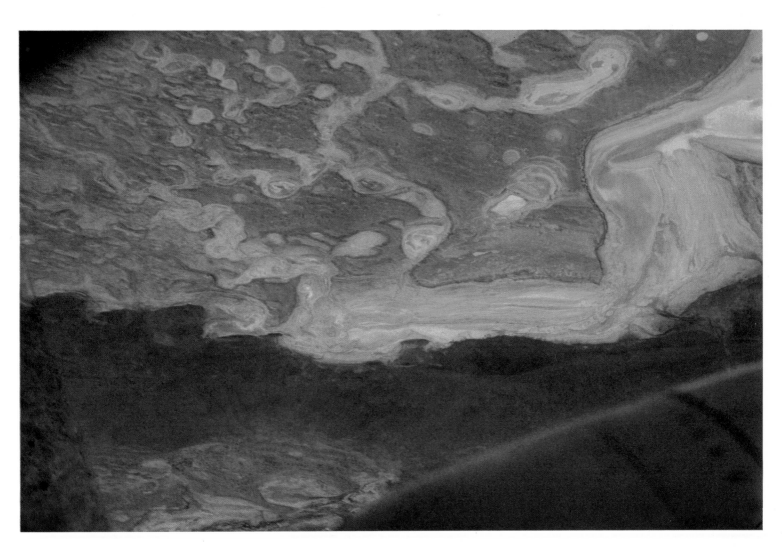

Dry river course, central Australia.

unsuspected by the quick-witted city people they encounter.

There is an extra cunning in the humour of the country German Australians amongst whom I was brought up, north of the Barossa Valley in South Australia. Their families have been in Australia for more than 100 years, but many of them still have a rich German accent. There was a huge German named Schubert who worked as a share-farmer at Anlaby, the old sheep station where I was born. One day, the bookkeeper asked the farmer: *Are you any relation to the famous composer?* Schubert looked down at him and said in his heavy accent, *Ach! So you have heard of him also?*

I also like the earthiness and irreverence of country humour, common to both the boss and the stockman, as work and dirty hands are. I remember a station owner, a grazier, who had been down to a garden-party at Government House, saying, *Those society women rattle with jewellery like an old daggy ewe.*

The mixture of coarseness, tenderness and a directness that can be mistaken for cruelty is characteristic of Australian country people. I have heard a farmer who is as gentle as a mother with his cows and calves talking about shooting foxes: *I saw a couple of them in the quarry paddock, the dog was on the vixen, mating her. When they saw me coming in the ute they lit off, they went sideways for 100 yards, four-legged, with him still on till I got close enough to blow him off.*

Another time we were loading 300 old ewes on to a semi-trailer, in the pouring rain that still had not broken the drought. The old ewes stood with drooping necks and hipbones like the Himalayas, as if they knew they would fetch only 40 cents each. The young truck driver cursed with nonstop profanity at the ewes for their weak stubbornness and at his over-excited dogs and *those bloody city union bastards at the meatworks, they get $50 a day for handing the tea round. I've worked both city and country, I know who the bludgers are.* Amongst the ewes there was a little lamb born after shearing, with its mother, and the truck driver said, *Can I have him, he'll never make it otherwise. My little boy loves to bring them up. He got $2 for the wool off the one he has now.* He popped it into the cage on the side of the truck together with his dogs, Trixie and Jake. *They won't do him any harm.*

The Australian earth is always in an intimate, often a desperate, relation with the other three elements. It is usually short of water, sometimes flooded; it is blown away by winds from the furnace of the Centre; it is scorched, sometimes deliberately, by fire.

For a long time the land was brutally treated by Australians. Of all the countries of the world, only Australian earth had never been impacted by the hooves of animals, cattle, sheep, goats, pigs, and had never been turned in a furrow. In remote areas it is still easy to imagine that untouched land, even to share that childhood dream of a place on which no white man has ever set foot. Then came the graziers, who often overstocked (though not as often as some historians think), and the farmers who often ploughed up country, as in West and South Australia, that was basically too dry to make it safe to grow crops. When I was a boy it was a matter of snobbery to be a grazier rather than a farmer; a little of this still clings to pig farmers, who can sometimes be heard to call themselves graziers. I can remember at school, when we were asked to call out our fathers' occupations, how everyone laughed at a boy who called out *Farmer* when his father owned half a dozen cattle and sheep stations. (I can also remember giggles when one solemn boy gave his father's profession as *Gentleman*; something inconceivable nowadays.)

Today, except in the more arid or mountainous regions, graziers have to be farmers and farmers have to be graziers, since the land responds best to a rotation of cropping, pasture improvement with clovers and medics, and grazing. But basically sheep- and cattlemen still do not care for crops. The Australian merino, that wonderfully adaptable animal, can battle through droughts better than crops do, although it is true that blow-fly strike is even more nerve-wracking than the troubles of wet wheat. Certainly it is more unpleasant; there is no more revolting or piteous sight than a fly-blown sheep stumbling around unable to do anything about its stinking wool and the maggots that are boring their way into its flesh.

In 150 years there have been vast changes in sheep and cattle stations, both in human and scientific terms. Properties that would have had a dozen station hands and jackeroos now make do with one or none, with a man's wife and children doing the jobs.

The old diseases are mostly under control, except for flystrike, when the remedy is still palliative, and pastures are immeasurably improved, even if markets are not. But in that same 150 years nothing has changed in the basic relation of man and animal, even though the man may ride a motor cycle instead of a horse, and the shearer uses a handpiece instead of blades. Cattle milling in dusty yards or sheep streaming out through an open gate still look the same as they did in the old songs or in Lawson's stories or Paterson's poems.

On the land life does not come out new like a daily newspaper, everything is in constant motion, the seeds in the ground, the wool on the sheep, the calves growing. An extreme heat wave seems to paralyse everything.

The threat of fire nags all through every summer. In most of Australia for the last six months of the year fire is an acute hazard. Even in October a man burning-off in a lush Hobart suburb can start a bushfire in which houses are burnt to the ground. William Strutt's *Black Thursday* is a famous painting of the Victorian bushfires on 6 February 1851, when it was 117° in the shade in Melbourne at 11 a.m., and almost the whole state was alight from the Dandenongs to the South Australian border. What Strutt painted could have been true of a hundred later tragedies.

One of Australia's problems is that eucalypts in extreme heat seem to give off volatile gases, so that whole trees burst into flames before the actual fire has reached them. There is no better description of an Australian bushfire than Judge Stretton's succinct report of his Royal Commission on the January 1939 Victorian fires: *Seventy-one lives were lost. Sixty-nine mills were burned. Millions of acres of fine forest, of almost incalculable value, were destroyed or badly damaged. Townships were obliterated in a few minutes. Mills, houses, bridges, tramways, machinery, were burned to the ground; men, cattle, horses, sheep were devoured by the fires or asphyxiated by the scorching debilitated air . . . Steel girders and machinery were twisted by heat as if they had been of fine wire. Sleepers of heavy durable material, set in soil, their upper surfaces flush with the ground, were burnt through . . . Balls of crackling fire sped at a great pace in advance of the fires, consuming with a roaring, explosive noise all that they touched. Houses of brick were seen and*

Just after rain, near Mt Tom Price, Western Australia.

Vintage coming in, Saltram Winery, Angaston, South Australia.

heard to leap into a roar of flames before the fires had reached them . . . Such was the force of the wind that in many places hundreds of trees of great size were blown clear of the earth, tons of soil with embedded masses of rock still adhering to the roots; for mile upon mile, the former forest monarchs were laid in confusion, burnt, torn from the earth, and piled one upon another as matches strewn by a giant hand.

The scenario does not change. In 1976 vast areas of the rich grazing land of the Western District of Victoria, including whole towns, were obliterated. Every state of Australia has been through similar ordeals of fire, although in the north of Western Australia and in the Northern Territory the white man follows the ancient Aboriginal practice of burning the tall rank grass. For the Aborigines it flushed out the game; for the white man it brings up new green growth. But it is a perilous business when there is no possibility of controlling such fires, which may run for hundreds of square miles.

One such fire, lit by the Aborigines, nearly trapped my father in 1908 when he and Murray Aunger were driving the first car to cross Australia, from Adelaide to Darwin. There were, of course, no roads for them to follow, and no hope of getting away from the fire which swept all around them somewhat north of Tennant Creek. Their Talbot car was especially vulnerable because of the large amount of petrol it was carrying in spare cans. There is something particularly poignant in the conjunction of man's most ancient friend/enemy, the primitive practices of the Aborigines, and this first bumbling representative of the mechanical age, all coming together half way between Alice Springs and Darwin in some of the least inhabited country on earth. As it was, my father and Aunger survived, and drove on safely, if not without hazard, to Darwin.

Australia's emptiness, of course, makes it all the easier for bushfires; in many areas they just have to be left to burn themselves out, or be stopped by a change of wind. But there is also an ecological balance. Some Australian plants have seeds which germinate best when cracked by fire. Then, of course, they need water to make them grow.

Water, the fourth of the old elements, is synonymous in Australia with drought. This is particularly so in South Australia, where 78 per cent of the state is arid, and there is only one big river, the Murray, which has to be shared with New South Wales and Victoria. Pipelines from the Murray river run to Adelaide, and all across the central regions; without the Murray water, South Australia's economy would collapse.

Western Australia (which is six times as big as Texas) is even worse off than South Australia, containing more arid land without even one large river, except in the wild northern Kimberleys. Not quite so far north, in the cyclonic areas of Port Hedland, the annual rainfall of 10 to 15 inches may fall in a couple of days.

In Perth hotels there is a card appealing to the visitor to save water: *Western Australia has experienced drought conditions over the past two years and as a consequence the State now faces a severe water shortage.* It is a practical card, for it tells you how much water you use. *'Shower.' Wet down, soap up, rinse off. Say about three minutes. 30 litres or less. 'Bath.' May we suggest a shower. An average tub 70–90 litres. 'Washing Hands.' Place plug in basin NOT tap running. 3 litres.* And so on.

But perhaps the most incongruous thing about Australia is that its arid centre is more or less floating on what seems to be almost limitless water. The Australian artesian basins are the biggest in the world and lie under an area of more than a million square miles.

In 1879 Professor Ralph Tate, the first occupant of the Chair of Natural Sciences in the new University of Adelaide, reported on what he called the mound springs near Lake Eyre, which he was sure were surface manifestations of artesian water.

In the midst of the bleak and waterless semi-desert (for Lake Eyre, of course, is salt except when flooded), you suddenly come upon these mounds, which are as high as 50 feet. When you climb to the top there is an eye of water within the lashes of reeds, warm enough to swim in. But it is not easy on the nerves, especially if you remember the Aboriginal legends of the bunyip, the water monster, for every few minutes there is a rumble and a surge as a boil of water lifts and finally bursts, overflowing the banks and bringing up fresh green growth in the red and yellow landscape.

The artesian waters vary from time to time in their flow, but there is no evidence that they are running dry, despite the prodigious drain upon them of perhaps 8,000 bores with a daily flow of 350 million gallons. In the dry country you know you are on the way to a bore when you see water, usually hot, flowing down an open drain (with a loss from soakage and evaporation of perhaps 10,000 gallons a day). Then you come on the bore, a great gout of water spouting untended, often with a fence around it and a notice *Danger!* The notice is necessary; sometimes the water is nearly boiling. On a recent visit to north-west Western Australia we were told that a young man had ignored the signs at a bore and had been boiled alive after jumping into the pool. Some of the bores are more than 6,000 feet deep; others provide abundant water at 200 feet.

Australia's one great river system is the Murray, joined by the Lachlan, the Murrumbidgee and the Darling, and other smaller rivers. It irrigates Mildura, Renmark and all the other green areas along its dry course; it provides Adelaide with its repulsive drinking water; it keeps alive towns like Port Augusta and Whyalla; and it flows out in a tiny channel into the surf of the Southern Ocean. Its waters, though somewhat polluted and threatened by salt seepage, are still noble, and its fish still to be caught, though fishing has suffered since the accidental introduction of the European carp, one of those pests that proliferate in Australia, like the rabbit and a thousand weeds. The paddlesteamers of the Murray and Darling once made it a great waterway, but they were put out of business by road and rail transport.

One of the surest ways to penetrate into the heart of Australia, to explore it at peace and in depth, is to hire a houseboat from one of the towns along the river, and just slowly let the paddle-wheel take you out of reach of rush, noise, dirty air, telephones, TV and, if you wish, people. For days on the river you may speak to no one and see not a soul except a fisherman checking his drum nets. I remember our fury when our peace was disrupted by another houseboat that pulled into the bank alongside us. *I wonder*, said an apologetic man, *if you could spare us some bread. We thought there would be some shops along the river.* Fortunately, there are none, and only

birds and kangaroos watch from the banks as the river winds through its huge old red gums.

At first there is an apparent monotony, grey-brown banks, brown river, white gums, dun leaves. Then it becomes endless variety. Every single gum is different. They are so anthropomorphic they would have driven the ancient Greeks mad, bringing their myths to life with slender girls and heavy, warty old men. Against these fantasies the bark offers infinite abstract patterns of white and grey, green and brown. The birds are always beside you in all their varieties; teal, woodduck, pink eye and the most handsome of all, the mountain duck. In their quick, banking flight they rise far from the slow sweep of pelicans, the urgent ripple of black swans, the fuss of waterhens. A huge wedge-tailed eagle is hotly pursued by crows, then by a whistling eagle defending his territory, then by magpies zooming like fighters.

At evening you tie up by a long lagoon where foxes and kangaroos come to drink. Under the slenderest new moon the silence is almost total, except for a little whirr of water where the paddle-wheel is slowly turned by the water, the only sign of all that immense volume moving towards the sea. At dawn the currawongs call, rounded and clear, almost a melody but never quiet.

Astonishingly enough, all this peace and quiet releases a Rabelaisian rortiness amongst the people who hire the houseboats, judging from the ships' logs which they write up, throwing all their inhibitions into the river, recording their sex lives and their herculean boozing sessions and their happy ineptitude as river boatmen. The houseboats must be tough, judging by the number of times the crews run them aground or high and dry on snags. (There is an emergency radio if you get hopelessly stuck.)

There are lots of honeymooners. *Ventured upstream only about 2 miles due to passionate husband.* Next day: *Returned to 2 mile point, due to love-struck first mate. After breakfast and a lie down we once again set off upon the mighty waters.*

Other honeymoon wives were not so lucky. *Randy (literally) and*

Aftermath of bushfire, Tasmania.

Red kangaroo in spinifex.

crew Barbara ('1st'?? mate) moored near the town for a few nights and her worst suspicions were confirmed when *male mate of husband spent every night on board drinking till 2 a.m. Some honeymoon!*

There is heroic boasting about the amount of grog consumed. *Drunk? Blotto? Paraletic? Blind? Anebriated? What else do you expect with 15 dozen cases of beer on board. Yippee!!*

Some houseboaters, more solemn, almost make a life of it. A couple from Victoria had hired the houseboat for eight weeks and travelled 518 miles, making a total of 2,525 miles in houseboats over eight years.

The one place on the river where you can never take a houseboat is to the Murray Mouth, the channel of vicious rips that cuts through the 90 mile beach of the Coorong, that narrow strip of land and sandhills enclosing a lake alive with fish and birds, a haunting region unlike any other in Australia.

Seawater is almost a different element from fresh. While the river reflects the land, the ocean is its own world. Australians are lucky with the sea. All the capital cities and several other big towns and cities are on the sea. But they are not only ports, they are cities with marvellous beaches and crowded boat-harbours where anyone can be involved with the sea. There are no other sea-cities in the world quite like the Australian cities, the old wild scrub so close behind them, the wild ocean at their door.

Over all is the air. The Greek god Hermes, the messenger, with wings on his sandals, must take a special interest in Australia. The winds constantly bring messages, the scents of dry gum-leaves or flowering wattle, acrid messages of bushfire, red signals of dust, the blessed relief of the cool change from the sea.

The winds have names, some unprintable, like the searing northerlies that wither South Australia and Victoria in heat-waves; others banal, like Cyclone Tracy that destroyed the city of Darwin. Some are affectionate, like the Fremantle Doctor bringing relief to a sweltering Perth, or the southerly buster of the New South Wales coast, a violent swing of the wind to the south-west during spring and summer. Early Sydney settlers called it a brickfielder, as it swamped the city in dust from the southerly brickworks. Willy-willies are spirals of dust and dry vegetation that wander across the red plains of the interior in summer. They are capricious and unpredictable, sometimes 200 feet high. Hang on to your hat or wind up the windows of the car if they swerve towards you. Up in the north-west there is a ferocious local squall, a giant willy-willy turned angry, called a cock-eyed bob.

In Australia the air, which belongs to no one, has in fact made an incalculable contribution to the people's sense of belonging. The aeroplane has not only brought Australians together but allayed their fears of the outside world. When I was a boy in the 1930's it took over a month for a ship to reach London. Very few passenger ships went across the Pacific, and even fewer to China or Japan or Singapore. Through the P. & O. and Orient Line ships the emphasis was heavily British, the destination always London. The aeroplane has changed all this. London is late on a list that begins with Bali, and America is every day.

As for the Outback and the North, one of the greatest humane achievements of Australian history has been the Flying Doctor service. Isolation has also been made infinitely less lonely by the aeroplane. If the land has shaped Australian life, then the air has unexpectedly nourished it.

It is fitting that some of the great pioneers of aviation, Lawrence Hargrave, Kingsford Smith, C. Ulm, P.G. Taylor, Hudson Fysh, Horrie Miller, have been Australians. My first flight was in a Gipsy Moth of Horrie Miller's sitting in the front seat on my brother Dick's lap. Later, Horrie flew up to Anlaby in his single-engined Fokker, landed in a paddock, and took us over to Port Victoria to look at the last of the sailing ships loading grain for Europe. We flew past the forest of masts and yards of those wonderful slender ships, *Herzogin Cecilie, Passat, Pamir, Lawhill*; it was the end and the beginning of two eras in Australian history. The sailing ships were the last descendants of the great windjammers, the clipper ships that reached Australia in just over 60 days, *Lightning, Thermopylae, Cutty Sark*. The Port Victoria fleet were going back to Europe around Cape Horn, a voyage of about 110 days. Horrie's Fokker was no record-breaker, but only a year before, the Melbourne Centenary Air Race from London had been won by Campbell Black and C.W.A. Scott in a DH Comet in 71 hours, and not far behind them was a standard Douglas airliner, with passengers, of the Royal Netherlands Indies Airways (KNILM).

With the air goes light, and Australia's light is one of its unmistakable characteristics. When a painter like Sidney Nolan comes home to Australia after years abroad you can almost feel the glow in him as he looks at the gum trees against the sky and the galahs tumbling, grey, pink and rose, out of the branches. The fact that landscape is a major and enduring subject in Australian painting is as much a tribute to the light as to the landscape, as witness the work of painters as different as Streeton, Roberts, Gruner, Heysen, Nolan, Arthur Boyd and Fred Williams. But it does not need a painter's eye to apprehend this extraordinary quality of Australian light. It is not just that the air is mostly free of smog, but that the dryness gives a purity to the light that is absent from the skies of damper countries. The desert is said to be harsh, and so it is in terms of its capacity to kill. But in terms of light and distance it is exceedingly delicate. And even in the cities there is a rare quality to the light, different in each city.

If one is writing in praise of Australian light, then one must also write of darkness. Not the absence of light, but the presence of the stars; not only the largesse of those visible from the southern hemisphere, but the clarity with which they shine through the Australian air. As with the pioneering aviators, it is pleasant to know that some of the most important astronomical research in the world is being done in Australia, especially at the Australian National University and the radio telescope installations at Parkes and Siding Springs.

Air, light and birds – one cannot think of one without the others. David Campbell, a poet, farmer and wartime pilot, was familiar as only a poet, a farmer and a pilot can be with the air and what goes on across the earth beneath. A poem of his, *Windy Gap*, is the most perfect expression I know of the clarity of Australian light, and the winds that are part of it.

As I was going through Windy Gap
A hawk and a cloud hung over the map.

The land lay bare and the wind blew loud
And the hawk cried out from the heart of the cloud.

'Before I fold my wings in sleep
I'll pick the bones of your travelling sheep,

'For the leaves blow back and the wintry sun
Shows the tree's white skeleton.'

A magpie sat in the tree's high top
Singing a song on Windy Gap

That streamed far down to the plain below
Like a shaft of light from a high window.

From the bending tree he sang aloud,
And the sun shone out of the heart of the cloud

And it seemed to me as we travelled through
That my sheep were the notes that trumpet blew.

And so I sing this song of praise
For travelling sheep and blowing days.

Aboriginal children fishing, Northern Territory.

Australian boy in Greek district of Collingwood, Melbourne.

People

Until recently in Australia, perhaps even now in some unrepentant junk-shop, you could buy garden ornaments in the shape of Aborigines, like the gnomes or flamingoes made for suburban lawns. They were a perfect symbol of what most Australians wished for the Aborigines: the nomad immobilized by the goldfish pool of suburbia, without rights or needs.

Less than 20 years ago the Sydney *Bulletin* was still flying the slogan *Australia For The White Man* from its editorial mast. The *Bulletin* was concerned with keeping out the Chinese, Indians, Japanese and Negroes. The Aborigines did not count. At the same time the magazine was still running jokes of Aborigines saying things like *Me trackem feller plurry good, boss*. It also carried a page of anecdotes headed *Aboriginalities*, always with the same little drawing of an old Aborigine in rags and a top hat grilling a goanna over a fire.

Fortunately there have always been some white men in Australia who were neither racist nor indifferent, and who had no illusions about the benefits of civilization. The explorer Edward John Eyre's *Manners and Customs of the Aborigines of Australia*, written in 1845, was the first full account of the Aborigines based on systematic knowledge. His defence of these wronged and, at that time, despised people is one of the finest and most eloquent, and least known, of all the books written about the Aborigines. What he wrote is still, alas, true:

> *Daily and hourly do their wrongs multiply upon them. The more numerous the white population becomes, and the more advanced the stages of civilization to which the settlement progresses, the greater are the hardships that fall to their lot and the more completely are they cut off from the privileges of their birthright. All that they have is in succession taken away from them – their amusements, their enjoyments, their possessions, their freedom – and all that they receive in return is obloquy, and contempt, and degradation, and oppression.*

Twenty years after Eyre's comments, the Catholic Archbishop Polding wrote: *The unfortunate natives are indeed to be pitied . . . Alas! the march of European civilization is the march of desolation, and unless means are used which Liberals repudiate, the black savage will be exterminated to make place for a white savage – far more ruthless.*

Eyre and Polding represented a conscience which most Australians ignored. When Anthony Trollope visited Australia in 1871 it was quietly assumed that the Aborigines were a dying race; Trollope thought this the best thing that could happen. Sixty years later, when I was at school, the Aborigines might have died out for all that we were taught about them, and for all that our elders talked about them. It seems to be very different today; Australians are very conscious of the Aborigines, their wrongs and their hopes. But few really understand their predicament, and even fewer have actually met and talked to an Aborigine.

Yet the Aborigines have been here for 25,000 or 30,000 years. There was never any question of them either loving or hating Australia. They were Australia, and Australia was them, their culture, their legends, their bark and rock paintings, their Dreaming. W.E.H. Stanner, the white man who has written the best short account of the Dreaming, says: *It is a cosmogony, an account of the begetting of the universe, a story about creation. It is also a cosmology, an account or theory of how what was created became an orderly system. To be more precise, how the universe became a moral system. The white man could only offer in exchange the Book of Genesis, but there was never any suggestion that Adam and Eve were Aborigines.*

Stanner points out that neither time nor history has any relevance to the Dreaming, or indeed any meaning for the Aborigines. He writes, *The blacks sense this difficulty. I can recall one intelligent old man who said to me, with a cadence almost as though he had been speaking verse:*

'White man got no dreaming,
Him go 'nother way.
White man, him go different,
Him got road belong himself.'

The Aboriginal society which the white man destroyed had a number of virtues which white society is still trying to achieve. The Aborigines did not damage the country they lived in; they had art, dance and songs that gave the land and their life meaning; they had no formal chiefs and thus no power struggles; they did not know the envy of want or the worry of money. They had violent fights, but no organized wars. Life was not idyllic, especially for women, but it had shape, depth and structure.

Some of the worst damage to Aboriginal society was done in the name of 'protection'. The various State Aboriginal Protection Acts decreed amongst other things that Aborigines with children should be brought into settlements to be educated. All Aborigines bitterly resented the restrictions on their liberties imposed by these Settlements. It was a crime to 'escape' from them. How these Settlements destroyed the fabric of Aboriginal society is movingly shown in *The Two Worlds of Jimmie Barker*, a book by Janet Mathews based on conversations with an aged Aborigine.

Jimmie Barker had spent a happy if sometimes precarious childhood wandering with his tribe and with his half-caste mother, who had been left with her two children by their German-Australian father. At 11 he was forced to receive religious instruction from a preacher who said, *I do not want to be thought a good fellow by you people. I have just come to teach you heathens the way of Christ.* Jimmie Barker says that before he listened to this preacher and others like him, *I had always thought the world was wonderful; I had no idea that we were lower and worse than everyone else.*

In more than 20 years at the Brewarrina Settlement he knew only one good manager. Housing was appalling. With the beautiful Barwon river at their door they were not allowed vegetable gardens, and water had to be carted up the steep banks in buckets. The manager strode around cracking a stockwhip at the children. The old legends and traditions on which he had been brought up were broken. *The manager told us straight out we were just 'nothing' . . . The public had no idea the way we were forced to live.*

The very virtues of Aboriginal society meant that it lacked immunity not only to the diseases but to many of the characteristics of white society. Aggression, greed, egotism, pragmatism and a sense of racial superiority were as deadly as syphilis or influenza. The imposition of the white man's law caused unfathomable complications. The Aborigines, caught between two codes of right and wrong, have often ended with neither, in total and debilitating confusion. The Aborigines were often willing helpers in the slaughter of their own race; the Native Police in Queensland and Victoria were especially ferocious.

The good life . . . horizontal.

The good life . . . vertical.

There is no evading the crimes which white Australians have committed against the Aborigines. Those recorded are numerous enough, but for every one of those there are 100 vanished skeletons of men, women and children, shot or poisoned with flour or dead of drink or disease or simply the loss of the will to live.

Australia is far behind the USA or Canada or New Zealand in the matter of land rights and educational, medical and housing arrangements for the natives of the country. Those sympathetic white men like Dr. H.C. Coombs who have been most involved with Aborigines over the years are adamant that no solution will be found until the Aborigines are allowed to run their own affairs.

Certainly a tribe, or clan, can be saved from being ruined by alcohol if the Elders refuse to allow it on the settlement, and if whites are prevented from selling it to them. A resort owner near Alice Springs was convicted on such a charge in late 1978.

But it is not only the white men who sell liquor in dry areas. (It is sadly ironic that the change in law which allowed Aborigines to drink in bars was, and is, regarded as a blow against discrimination.) A cattle station owner in the Northern Territory, who has always had excellent relations with his black station hands, told me of a recent episode at his camp, which is dry. The offender, an Aborigine from the local town some 80 miles away, had brought out 12 cartons, each containing four half-gallon flagons of port, and was selling them at three times their normal price.

Alcohol both epitomizes contemporary white good will towards the Aborigines, and hints at the backlash that follows. The hard old maxim that you don't know a man until you've got drunk with him works exactly back to front with ordinary shocked Australians, from the cities and the south, who see Aborigines drunk. They don't know them sober.

Ignorance is the basis of Australian, or any other, racism. But the breaking down of that ignorance is a two-way affair. Aborigines no longer want assimilation; they want to preserve their own traditions.

With the development of land rights and self-determination, white and black children will grow up quite separately, each ignorant of the other's culture. This sounds like a sort of apartheid, but it bears no relation to the South African variety, as Aborigines and whites in Australia have equal rights in law – at least in theory. And in most everyday affairs.

But Aboriginal land rights are another matter, and the law is still confused between States and Commonwealth, and in the extent of the Aboriginal claim to rights. In April 1979 the Aborigines lost a High Court case in which they claimed that the whole of Australia belonged to them since they had been unlawfully dispossessed of their lands. Mr. Justice Gibbs said: *The annexation of the east coast of Australia by Captain Cook in 1770, and the subsequent acts by which the whole of the Australian continent became part of the dominions of the Crown, were acts of state whose validity cannot be challenged . . . The contention that there is in Australia an Aboriginal nation exercising sovereignty, even of a limited kind, is quite impossible in law to maintain. It is fundamental to our legal system that the Australian colonies became British possessions by settlement and not by conquest.*

Settlement. Conquest. The law may split its hairs, but the historian is entitled to draw his own conclusions. There have been three, perhaps four, stages in the history of the occupation of the land. The first, the Aboriginal, went back beyond recorded history and yet still remains, for the mythical totemic ancestors are present in the lives of the Aborigines, their footprints on a rock, their wanderings in a river. The second stage was of settlement without treaty (which according to law is not conquest) by the British. The land was subdued, as far as drought and bushfires would ever allow, and it was cursed rather than cosseted. The Aborigines were dispossessed. The third stage came when roots went down into Australian soil, when children grew up on land their fathers had cleared, and even though people might still politically be 'loyal' to Britain, there was no doubt of their loyalty to their own land. There is a fourth stage, I think, which exists but is scarcely recognized. This involves the love that city people have learned for the land of Australia, the sense of belonging that sets them wandering in their cars and caravans and camper-vans all over Australia.

There is a curious and illogical link between the first and last wanderers. The Aborigines were nomads for economic reasons, following game or seasonal fruits. The white Australians today wander for spiritual reasons, to satisfy their souls both with discovery and belonging. Yet the Aborigines were also on a journey of the soul, because for them the land existed primarily in spirit, never for mere economic survival.

There is no evidence that the Aborigines fought wars of systematic territorial aggression. Nor did the white invaders fight wars with the Aborigines to take their land. It happened piece by piece, as the pastoral stations extended. The British Government dispatched settlers for Australia with high notions of respecting Aboriginal land rights. South Australia, the one free state, was founded on the best moral principles. However, no land was set aside for the Aborigines nor was compensation paid to them for the loss of the land. What followed was what W.E.H. Stanner has called *a cult of forgetfulness practised on a national scale.*

The great awakening of the Australian consciousness in the past 25 years disturbed this forgetfulness, although not quite with the shock of an alarm ringing. Legislation was passed for civil and political rights for the Aborigines, and a Referendum was approved (a rare thing in Australia) by a 90 per cent majority, giving the Commonwealth power to legislate for all Aborigines in Australia. The recommendations of the Royal Commission conducted by Mr. Justice Woodward in 1973 and 1974 into land rights were accepted by all major political parties, and embodied in the Aboriginal Land Rights (Northern Territory) Act. In 1978 similar conclusions were embodied in a report on Pitjantjatjara Land Rights presented to the South Australian Government.

The South Australian report recognizes the Aboriginal relation to the land, and, in accordance with national Aboriginal Affairs policy, *the need to acknowledge, and then act upon, an ethic of restitution, returning as much as reasonably possible of the land alienated from the Aborigines in the settlement of the country.*

Anticipating the criticism that was about to descend upon them, the Working Party who prepared the report continued: *After having said that, we are conscious that many people would find such resort to 'simple justice' unconvincing principally because it goes hand in hand*

Barbecues supplied by Melbourne City Council, River Yarra.

War and peace in Canberra.

with what is seen to be a glaring omission on the part of the Aboriginals themselves: that is their almost total uninterest in using the land 'productively'.

As late as March 1979 the Australian Mining Industry Council and the Stockowners Association of South Australia were still attacking the notion of Aborigines having land right privileges not available to white Australians. The Pitjantjatjara lands occupy an enormous area in the centre of Australia, extending into Western Australia.

And the President of the Stockowners' Association of South Australia was saying: *In general, once Aborigines are given land they don't know what to do with it. They lack the expertise, ability and, above all, the motivation to do anything to make the land produce.*

Nothing could more clearly illustrate the unfathomable abyss between white and Aboriginal concepts of the use of land. But the problem still has to be faced that, although for 30,000 years the Aborigines made what they considered good use of the land, they are not going to go back to their old ways. They are not going to abandon their cars, tinned food and radios and go back to hunting, even with rifles. And if their land is not going to be made productive, they are going to have to exist on Government handouts.

Even when traditions are observed, their implementation depends on money. When we were at Groote Eylandt in Arnhem Land a shuttle service of aircraft was flying the Aborigines out, some to continue by air and others by four-wheel-drive vehicles, to a tribal gathering at Millingimbi, 200 miles away.

Sometimes the traditions have collapsed. In the Kimberleys one station owner, whose family have always had exceptionally good relations with the Aborigines, recalled hunting expeditions in the old days (30 years ago). All the blacks would get out of their shirts and moleskins and go off in a procession with their spears and boomerangs, followed by the women carrying all the rest of the gear. On Sunday they would return, happy and successful, the hunters springing along with their weapons, the women trudging along behind laden down with kangaroos and wallabies.

Now, she said to us, *it's into the town, to the pub. You saw them as you drove in.*

In theory, when Aborigines are running their own stations they will be able to stop the drinking. On Peppimenarti in the Northern Territory, for instance, those living on the station are entitled to buy four cans of beer a day.

Peppimenarti, and Mimili in South Australia, are examples of stations where the Aborigines intend to run enterprises like the white man's, and eventually be self-supporting. Stewart Harris, who has written one of the best and most sympathetic books about the Aborigines, *This Our Land*, is very hopeful for the future of Peppimenarti, even though the Department of Aboriginal Affairs is at present injecting $250,000 a year into its economy. Other Aboriginal-run stations are not so promising. In the far north-west of Western Australia I asked about a nearby sheep station, the amalgamation of two formerly white-owned stations. There were two problems. One was that young Aborigines would not leave the town to go out and work on the station. The other was that there was no shearing in 1978. The reason was that all 7,000 sheep on the station had been eaten.

The backlash is already apparent in the North and West, where whites consider the blacks subsidized beyond reason. One sometimes suspects that Southern whites, especially around Canberra, are expiating their guilt over the past treatment of Aborigines in an orgy of giving, as if this will mean forgiving. Of course it will not, especially as there is some doubt as to where all the money goes (about $200 million from the Federal Government and from the States).

On a recent journey to the North-West and Northern Territory I was told several unpleasant stories about whites and blacks co-operating to make off with monies intended for Aboriginal welfare. That is a relatively simple matter of crime, and, eventually, punishment. But there are also unpunishable crimes. Recently the Minister and a plane-load of VIPs flew up from Canberra for the unveiling of a new million-dollar hospital in the Kimberleys. When it was over, the Minister, radiating virtue, presented the local Aborigines with a cheque for $60,000 to build a night basketball ground. But they already had three basketball grounds, one with lights, and were not using any of them.

Although most discussion about the Aborigines' future centres upon land rights and self-determination, this ignores the large number of urban Aborigines. They have come to the cities for reasons of security, employment, health and education, and it is hard to believe they will return to the land. Professor Fay Gale, who has written a book called *Urban Aborigines*, comes to the final and disturbing conclusion that: *The city appears to offer Aborigines the kind of economic and social environment in which they can achieve self-sufficiency and equality, on their terms, for perhaps the first time since European colonization.* I like the comment of one Aborigine who said to Professor Gale: *The city gives us the chance to educate the white man to see that we are not as stupid as he thinks.*

Of course there are also those who fail in the city, and can be seen drunk on methylated spirits sleeping on park benches, as in Jack Davis's haunting poem, *Desolation*.

We are tired of the benches, our beds in the park,
We welcome the sundown that heralds the dark.
White lady methylate!
Keep us warm and from crying.
Hold back the hate
And hasten the dying.

But whether city Aborigines are desperate or successful, it is important to remember that they are not just city Aborigines. They are members of kin groups living in a city, 'Flinders Ranges people' or 'Oodnadatta people' living in Adelaide. Aborigines take their country with them wherever they go.

The presence of the Aborigines always made nonsense of the White Australia Policy. Even so, *Australia for the White Man* was not a sentiment shared by the British Government, either at the foundation of Australia or 100 years later. Sir Joseph Banks, who sailed with Cook, thought that Australia's proximity to Asia would be a great advantage, as cheap labour would be available. The convicts made this unnecessary. Later on, the Secretary of State for the Colonies was furious when Victoria in 1855, and New South Wales in 1861, passed Acts restricting Chinese immigration. *Exceptional legislation intended to exclude from any part of Her Majesty's*

The uniform of croquet.

Best foot forward at bowls.

Dominions the subjects of a State at peace with Her Majesty is highly objectionable in principle.

But those impeccable sentiments were set aside in the aftermath of rioting on the goldfields. With the arrival in five years of about 40,000 industrious Chinese, in Victoria alone, the colonists were talking of the presence of an 'inferior race' becoming a 'sore' that could turn into a 'plague'. Then the scare died down, the acts were repealed and for 10 years there were no restrictions on the immigration of non-European people to the Australian colonies.

The Palmer gold rush in the far north of Queensland brought it all to a head again. By 1877 there were 17,000 Chinese to 1,400 whites in the district, and nearly all the Chinese were male adults. Queensland then passed a Chinese Immigration Act similar to that passed by New South Wales in 1861. Fear of the Chinese was not peculiar to Australia. In the arguments preceding the passage of the Queensland Act enthusiasts quoted the United States Commissioners' report on the Chinese in California, which claimed that Chinese immigration had shown itself to be *ruinous to our labouring classes, promotive of caste, and dangerous to free institutions.*

By the 1890's the feeling had spread through all the colonies that people who were 'alien' and who stayed alien, especially when they worked harder and for lower wages than white Australians, should be excluded from immigrating. The Labor Party was for many years the staunchest supporter of a White Australia. Meanwhile the British Government continued to be displeased at these distinctions which were *contrary to the general conceptions of equality which have been the guiding principle of British rule throughout the Empire.* The *Bulletin's* rebuttal was to describe the British Empire as *the greatest nigger empire in the world* and to extol the blessings for a White Australia. *A White Australia will never have to fry a nigger at the stake.*

The White Australia Policy never *officially* existed. It was in fact contained in the Commonwealth Immigration Restriction Act which prohibited the entry of anyone who could not take a dictation test of 50 words in a European language. Those who framed the Act had in mind to keep out the 'poorer type' of European as well as 'the coloured races'. It could even be used to keep out highly intelligent Europeans, as in the famous case of Egon Kisch, a suspected Communist, who was given a dictation test in Gaelic.

The ideal was to make Australia a country of equal social conditions, of decent living and fair wages for all, and especially to preserve its British character. When Alfred Deakin was Prime Minister in 1903 he said, *The White Australia Policy goes down to the roots of our national existence.*

But the roots were nourishing a tree, and the tree was Australia, not Britain. Within 50 years it was strong enough to shelter millions of non-British migrants, many of them 'coloured'. Viewed cynically, Australia was lucky to have had the White Australia Policy. There is no Negro problem, no Indian problem, no Chinese problem – only an Aboriginal problem. But the policy imposed considerable damage on the racial morality of Australians, and on the image of Australia in the eyes of the world.

The impact of post-World War II immigration on Australian society is a complex one. There has been a revolutionary change in the composition of the Australian population, which since 1945 has absorbed nearly three and a half million migrants, the greatest population change in such a time span of any country in the world. Melbourne is now the third largest Greek-speaking city in the world, after Athens and Salonika. One quarter of the six million children born in Australia since the 1950's have at least one parent born overseas.

It is partly the presence of these children that has removed the old Australian prejudice against migrants. Until late in the 1940's refugees from Europe were still 'bloody reffos'. The Estonians, Latvians, Lithuanians, Scandinavians, Russians and Poles were 'bloody Balts'. They were following after the 'bloody Poms' (who first settled the country!) and the 'bloody Krauts, Dagoes and Chinks'.

Fortunately not all Australians had such attitudes, and many were happy to talk to the European migrants whose standards derived from civilizations that Australians knew only through books.

The Cultural Cringe, a deadly phrase coined by the Melbourne critic A.A. Phillips, has been an over-simplification when applied to many Australians of integrity. True, we lacked confidence in our own style, and still do; but at the same time we badly needed a sense of quality, the measurement of which can only come from an acquaintance with excellence. It is the classic dilemma of the provincial.

The more deplorable aspects of provincialism were all too obvious, especially in the late 1930's and '40's, in the treatment by the Australian Medical Association of doctors who were refugees from Hitler. Distinguished medical men with degrees from ancient European Universities were forced, if they wished to practise in Australia, to go back to medical school at an Australian University. In one celebrated case, in Adelaide, a Viennese doctor found himself among students studying a translation of one of his own text books!

Unfortunately the issue is not dead. A 1979 Government report found that, *Almost all groups of non-English speaking origin expressed concern at non-recognition of qualifications. Croatians and Italians who had worked in Germany and Switzerland compared Australian acceptance of qualifications unfavourably with Germany . . . Chileans commented that 'we had to have a trade qualification to get accepted for emigration to Australia but when we got here our qualifications are not recognized.'* A union official commented, *Unions, 70 to 80 per cent of whose members are migrants, have no one who can communicate with them.* Another said, *Most Turkish working women do not even know the name of their employer.*

This provincialism, and laziness, is part of Australia's British heritage, akin to the English belief that foreigners start across the Channel. In Australia's defence, it has all happened very rapidly. When one thinks how long ago in the 19th century a similar process began in the USA, a mere 30 years falls into place. The true effects of the great non-British migration to Australia are only just beginning to show.

Numerous examples come to mind. Franco Belgiorno-Nettis, an Italian engineer, arrived penniless in 1951. Before he could marry his wife, he had to wait eight months until he had enough money to pay for her passage from Italy. He is now managing director of Transfield, a company which put up the power lines over the mountains for the Snowy River scheme; Transfield has about a dozen subsidiaries ranging from engineering and construction to light aircraft and wine-making. Belgiorno-Nettis set up a bronze foundry to aid sculptors, then for years gave a most generous art prize for Australians; he now funds the Sydney Biennale of sculpture.

I remember when the Nossal family arrived during World War II as Austrian refugees from Nazi Germany; mutual friends had given them letters to my mother. Their youngest son is now Sir Gustav Nossal, Director of the Walter and Eliza Hall Institute of Medical Research, and one of the world's most distinguished immunologists, whose influences and activities in Australia go far beyond science.

Rudy Komon, a Czech journalist born in Vienna, arrived in Australia in 1950 at the age of 42. By 1958 he had established the art gallery in Sydney that bears his name; Komon not only has some of the best artists in Australia on his books, but through enlightened self-interest he paid the living expenses of many of them while they were establishing their names. He is also one of the most sought-after wine judges in Australia.

One of the migrants who has done most to help other migrants is the Queensland Director of Works, Roman Pavlyshen, who has made an extraordinary success of his life. Gino Merli, who runs the Milano, the best restaurant in Brisbane, is one of thousands of Europeans who have transformed Australians' eating and drinking habits.

In Adelaide in the 1930's the best place to eat, apart from a couple of hotels, was the Covent Garden Café. It served an incomparable mixed grill or crayfish with mayonnaise, but the menu did not extend much further, and of course there was no wine list, since no restaurants in Adelaide were licensed. But the amazing development of Australians' drinking tastes from malted milks and sarsaparilla to some of the best wine in the world cannot be explained just in terms of the migrants' influence. The migrant influx into the USA did not turn Americans into wine drinkers. I think it is due to the suggestibility that is an essential part of the easy-going, pleasure-loving Australian character. In the 1950's

Waiting for fish . . . Sydney.

Waiting for tram . . . Melbourne.

and '60's Australians travelled in millions to Europe and saw how much more pleasant life could be with civilized eating and drinking; their open-mindedness led them to follow this up at home, in their own houses and in the restaurants burgeoning all over the country.

A fine tradition of wine-making already existed. Many of the best Australian vineyards have been operating for over 100 years. International judges have attested to the excellence of Australian wine. But, as usual, it was often the people at the top who were the slowest to acknowledge that anything Australian could be of quality; these people prefer the dubious distinction of hinting that they drink nothing but Chateau Latour and Schloss Johannisberg. In the early 1960's when an eminent American was taken to lunch at a city club, he complained to me that he had been offered nothing but French and German wine (though the club had a fine cellar of Australian wine).

The migrants have helped Australians to bridge the gaps in their own culture, but at the same time there are painful gaps left, particularly between the old and the young.

I heard recently of a Greek girl, a student at the University, who took her mother to three Australian films made by women. The films dealt with such subjects as homosexuality, rape and abortion. By the time they drove home the mother was hysterical over her daughter's lack of anguish at growing up in a country where such things were openly discussed. When her daughter stopped the car the mother rushed down the street screaming abuse. A man tried to help her, and she picked up a stone and threw it at him. When the daughter finally got her mother home her father joined in the barrage of curses and threats, with cries of *Why did we leave Greece to bring up our children in this Sodom and Gomorrah?* The daughter, a quiet, loving and talented girl, was devastated. The parents, of course, deserve a sympathy it is hard to feel. Their secure traditional values are threatened; their daughter, an assimilated Australian, has a different set of values, and does not feel threatened by them, but by her parents. It is a tragic story, not peculiar to Australia, but given an added poignancy by the pragmatic Australian acceptance of individual freedom of choice.

Lack of contact between national traditions means a lack of information. Australians do not understand what alarms or baffles migrants, because they do not understand what to expect or what is expected of them. This is despite the valiant efforts of people like Al Grassby, the Commissioner of Community Relations. A recent survey showed that the unions and the police are very bad at handling the communication problems of non-English speaking migrants.

The burden of helping cross the gap is thrown on children. Italians at Myrtleford in Victoria said, *Our children are our main source of information about Australia, also for filling in forms and solving problems.* These Italians had been in Australia for many years. There is a desperate need for a wider extension of ethnic radio and other forms of communication in the migrants' native languages.

Language is almost entirely one-way, as Australians have shown no aptitude for speaking other languages despite the fact that millions of Australians travel overseas. Because of Australia's isolation and distance even those who have learned to speak a foreign language soon lose it through lack of practice at home. This extends to the official level, from unions to Government, with some hilariously inept results.

A Melbourne tram has been carrying a huge advertising poster of a man drinking a cup of coffee with that look of ecstasy and inanity so common to visual advertising. Underneath his obviously Greek face was a sentence in Greek characters. Admirable, I thought, showing respect to Melbourne's large Greek population. Then I noticed that the instant coffee being advertised was labelled '*Turkish* coffee'. I doubt that this was a deliberate effort to heal the ancient feud between Greeks and Turks; at least in its naïveté it was a favourable comment on the peacefulness of Australian life.

A leaflet issued in Greek by the Taxation Department recently had 20 incorrect characters on its title page, including one which does not exist in the Greek alphabet. The Greek version of *Instructions on how to Fill in a Tax Return*, when translated back into English, read *Instructions on how to have Intercourse with a Tax Return*.

In 1956 Manning Clark, who has become Australia's most

distinguished historian, wrote an essay called *Re-writing Australian History*. In it he demolished some of the fashionable clichés of Australia as a cultural desert populated by well-fed barbarians basking in a radical tradition; most of them supposedly descended from virtuous convicts who were 'Village Hampdens', victims of an unjust society. In dropping what he called *these comforters of the past* he showed how diverse and full of dramatic conflict our past had been. It seemed to him that D.H. Lawrence had misjudged both democracy and Australia with his irate comments: *This is the most democratic place I have ever been in. And the more I see of democracy the more I dislike it.*

I had read that passage in Lawrence's letters some six years before, when we were staying with Lawrence's old friend and biographer Richard Aldington in the South of France. At that time, far away, it seemed a fair comment, reinforced by all I had thought I had discovered in the magical ruins of old Europe. Later, when I read Clark's essay, I wondered about his conclusion that history must have *some great theme to lighten our darkness — that, for example, the era of bourgeois liberalism, of democracy, and belief in material progress is over, and that those who defend such a creed are the reactionaries of today.*

But that is not at all what those three million migrants were thinking when they left Europe for Australia. They had had enough of great conflicts; they wanted democracy, free institutions and the material things of life.

The migrants have strengthened Australia's deep-grained conservatism. Most of them don't want to make trouble, here or anywhere else. The exception was the Vietnam war, the greatest internal upheaval in Australia's history. A large number of European migrants were refugees from communism, and they honestly believed that the Vietnam war was a fight against communism. In the days when my wife and I were handing out anti-war pamphlets on the steps of Parliament House in Adelaide, the only person who abused us was a Latvian in his 50's.

The inner life is no longer sanctified by public worship. No one, anywhere, is building cathedrals. But the enjoyment of life is no longer regarded as a crime against the spirit; the swimming pool has replaced the vale of tears. The migrants have taken Australians on at their own game and showed them how to enjoy life more, and not only in obvious ways such as food and drink. The great parks of Australian cities have come to life as never before. Where once there was only a snoozing alcoholic there are now families of Greeks and Italians. Festivals are everywhere – Latvian, Dutch, Greek, Italian, and, biggest of all, the German Barossa festival that goes on for a week. I was on a plane not long ago with an Austrian-Australian butcher from Adelaide who had supplied several tons of sausages, mettwurst and leberwurst to the Schützenfest in Darwin. Australians learn Greek dancing and Lebanese cooking. Musica Viva, founded by migrants, is the largest chamber music organization in the world. And so on.

Assimilation has been extraordinarily successful. Today, the diversity of multi-ethnic Australia exists and is constantly encouraged. Australians have learned some humility about non-British people. The tragic contrast is between the non-British migrants and the Aborigines; for the Aborigines separation, not assimilation, seems the only hope. The Poles or Spaniards do not want to lose their identity, but they are happy – or at least, resigned – that their children should become Australians. Not so the Aborigines, who are already Australians, but of another kind.

Making music . . . Adelaide.

. . . making friends, Adelaide.

Cities

Australia has a capital that is not a true city, and seven cities that consider themselves capitals. Moreover, Melbourne and Sydney, which are big cities in terms of population and enormous in terms of area, each thinks of itself as not only the local capital, but as the most important, most prestigious, and richest city in Australia.

Federation, which instituted the Commonwealth of Australia on 1 January 1901 (and temporarily allowed Melbourne the glory of being the capital), has never affected the capitals of the States. There may be arguments about centralism and States rights, but no one would argue with a South Australian about the 'capital' being Adelaide, or with a Tasmanian about Hobart. Admittedly Northern Queenslanders are not quite so keen about Brisbane, and there is also a rather feeble New England Movement to break away from New South Wales. In no Australian city is there a national focus of power and talent to correspond with New York.

This strong local sense in Australian cities even extends to the sea, as if Sydney people owned the water in the Harbour or the surf at Bondi, or Melbourne people Port Phillip Bay. Brisbane has its extensions of sea beyond its own muddy waters, so that 'our' beaches for Brisbane people run away to the South or to the North, a long distance from the city.

Sydney's shape was determined by the sea, and like the sea it lies open and glowing to the eye. When it rains in Sydney the water comes down in sheets, and in the ensuing humidity shoes grow mould in cupboards. But the Sydney you remember is a soft light on golden sandstone, the attack of the ocean, the shelter of the Harbour. Even the redbrick eastern suburbs, for all their self-enclosed rituals, are not far from some surf beach or inlet of the sea. No other city in the world has such an extraordinary profile. Look at a road map of Sydney and its suburbs. Start at the bottom, at Port Hacking; then to the north is Botany Bay and the Georges River; then Port Jackson and Sydney Harbour; then Middle Harbour; and finally Pitt Water; all of them breaking the city into complex patterns of water and land.

The ocean surf beaches and the hundreds of miles of indented bays are clustered with the evidence of pleasure. And all those thousands of moored yachts and dinghies are only the visible fringe; there are thousands more on trailers in the back yards of redbrick suburbia. There are also hundreds of people in Sydney who live in houses that can be reached only by boat.

True, the sea represents trade as well as pleasure, and Sydney is a great port. But the docks are at the back of the Harbour, and by the time a ship has reached them it has already been accepted as part of Sydney, just as Joern Utzon's Opera House sails on the Harbour. Even Sydney's huge National Park, Ku-ring-gai Chase, has a boat harbour in the middle of its scrubby hills.

Sydney people are the greatest gamblers in Australia and Australians are the greatest gamblers on earth. How well Utzon understood this, when he freed the Opera House from the stern squares and cubes of ordinary city buildings. And how suitable that it should have been financed through all its millions from the proceeds of lotteries.

Sydney is a permanent affront to the Protestant work ethic. Of course Sydney people work hard and have their share of mortal miseries but the city still makes its demand – Enjoy life! Perhaps there is also some historical compulsion here, providing a more sombre relationship with the sea. Sydney's past is as dark and cruel as the depths and voids of the ocean. The convict blood and sweat have vanished from the cut sandstone, but both the acceptance of cruelty and the necessity for compensatory pleasure were built into Sydney's history.

The anonymous writers of ballads knew this. They could be as bitter as the author of *Jim Jones*:

They'll flog the poachin' out of you,
out there in Botany Bay!

Or merry as the Irishman, fresh out of the stocks for assaulting a constable, waiting outside the gate of the Female Factory at Parramatta with a *half pint of Cooper's best gin* for Molly McGuigan, the girl he wants to marry, who has also been in the stocks for *beating her mistress, Mrs. Cox*:

But the lass I adore, the lass for me,
Is a lass in the Female Factory.

The tone of these ballads is a good deal more authentic than the stately poetics of Judge Barron Field, who wrote a sonnet in 1822 to celebrate the setting up of a plaque at Kurnell to mark the spot where Captain Cook and Joseph Banks first landed.

Fix then th' Ephesian brass. 'Tis classic ground.

It does not ring true, yet it ought to; it symbolizes the difficulty Australians have always had in celebrating solemn moments in their past. It is also doing its bit to perpetuate the myth that it was the British who discovered Australia (of course, denying altogether the prior rights of the Aborigines). Field calls Cook 'Our Columbus of the South', blithely ignoring the Spaniards Quiros and Torres who, making landfalls in the Pacific Islands, thought they had found 'Austrialia', and the Dutchmen, who from 1606 to 1642 did discover Australia, making many landfalls in Northern, Western and South Australia, and Van Diemen's Land. Barron Field was a highly educated man; he must certainly have been aware that Australia was known as New Holland, long before Captain Cook called it New South Wales. He might even have mentioned his fellow countryman, the buccaneer William Dampier, who was in Western Australia 82 years before 'Columbus' Cook landed at Stingray Bay, rechristened Botany Bay, to scrape the *Endeavour*'s foul bottom.

But Sydney has always been romantic. The poet-explorer W.C. Wentworth saw it through a picturesque haze, like the painter Conrad Martens, with its *wide square, stately mansion, lofty windmills* and the ships

Thickly planted o'er the glossy bay
Where Sydney loves her beauty to survey.

By the end of the 19th century writers were concerned with a more realistic Sydney, its cruelties no longer those of convict society but of Victorian capitalism. Victor Daley saw *the Woman at the Washtub working 'till fall of night* with *hands wrinkled white,* and he had a vision of her washing the blood of mankind's crimes.

Christopher Brennan wandered a Sydney where:

The yellow gas is fired from street to street
past rows of heartless homes and hearths unlit.

From the thirties . . .

. . . into the seventies, Collins Street, Melbourne.

Henry Lawson cursed the toadies who turned out to grovel for the Royal Visit in 1901:

There'll be royal times in Sydney for the Cuff and Collar Push . . .
You shall meet the awful Lady of the latest Birthday Knight —

(He is trying to be English, don't-cher-know?)

Lawson also wrote in his stories of another Push, the Larrikin gangs who went around beating up each other and Sydney citizens, and they were favourite subjects of Norman Lindsay and other black and white artists.

Although Streeton and other Australian impressionists painted the Sydney beaches, no modern artists or writers did Sydney justice until a Swiss, Sali Herman, painted its terraces and steps and buildings, and Kenneth Slessor, grandson of a German Professor of Pianoforte called Schloesser, celebrated its harbour in poetry.

I looked out of my window in the dark
At waves with diamond quills and combs of light
That arched their mackerel-backs and smacked the sand
In the moon's drench, that straight enormous glaze,
And ships far off asleep, and Harbour-buoys
Passing their fireballs wearily each to each . . .

In another poem, Captain Dobbin, retired from the South Seas, looks out from *Laburnum Villa*,

In whose blank windows the harbour hangs
Like a fog against the glass,
Golden and smoky, or stoned with a white glitter,
And boats go by, suspended in the pane,
Blue Funnel, Red Funnel, Messageries Maritimes,
Lugged down the port like sea-beasts taken alive . . .

That phrase *stoned with a white glitter* exactly expresses the light of Sydney, when the white terraces of houses seem to lift straight out of the distant smoky-blue water.

Sydney, like Hobart, is basically 18th century in its blend of classical harmony and balance with human dignity and brutality. The perfect symbol of this blend is the convict architect Francis Greenway, sentenced to death in Bristol in 1812 for forgery, but given 14 years in New South Wales in exchange for the gallows. With Governor Macquarie as patron, he designed some of the most beautiful early Australian buildings in Parramatta, Windsor and Sydney itself, but it is typical of Australia's under-confidence in the worth of its own treasures that many of Greenway's buildings were either mutilated or destroyed. The saddest casualty was his grandest design, the barracks and compound for male convicts in Queen's Square, Sydney, which is almost entirely lost. Only recently have Australians come to realize that the country's architectural heritage does not only consist in the actual buildings but in the fact that they embody the country's history.

All modern Western cities, especially those in Australia, are divided into the city itself, which is the sum of local history, and the suburbs, which are international and live in a perpetual present ceaselessly modified by the commands of advertising. There are islands of historical stone or brick, overtaken by suburbia, as in Parramatta, but these only make the distinction more obvious.

Australia's greatest living writer, Patrick White, once created a suburb of Sydney, Sarsaparilla, which exists in time no less surely than if it were in concrete and brick veneer.

White now lives near the heart of Sydney, but when he came back to Australia in 1951 after many years abroad, he settled in Castle Hill, now an outer suburb, which was then where the country began.

His Sydney is the nag and frenzy of daily-emptying suburbia, the gossip and the heat trapped in the endless boxes. It is also batty old ladies and decayed mansions, artists and musicians who achieve the city's homage when that is not what they need. But White is also a master of the tone and attitudes of Sydney's powerful and wealthy.

White himself is an Australian aristocrat, if such a being is allowed in a land of compulsory democracy, and he has the aristocrat's ability to talk to and understand anyone in any level of society. This is totally unlike the characteristic, easy-going Australian friendliness, in which every William is an instant Bill. White has the ability to see through Sydney's high society and its uneasy grandeur. He is the only Australian writer, with the exception of Martin Boyd, who can understand the manners and customs and pretensions of an upper class which has no confidence in being upper and no certainty of class.

In Sydney such people may be rich, and a European like Rudy Komon may have trained them in what paintings to buy and what wines to drink, but they are not well enough educated, they lack the intellectual rigour to be true leaders of society.

The beauty of Australian democracy is that there are as many cultivated and thoughtful people in suburbia as in the grander areas, and this gives a groundswell of true feeling that ignores the trendy surface breezes.

The symbol of Sydney is the Harbour Bridge, the ceaseless movement in and out, and below on the water. Melbourne, though just as big and busy, is more inward, deeply structured in parks and gardens, sheltered from the ocean, spread around the bay, easing off into the Dandenongs and other hills instead of fronting up to the wall of the Blue Mountains. Melbourne also has a convict past (like every Australian State except South Australia), but this is the product of a later age than Sydney, and Melbourne historically is a very Victorian city. The severity of the bluestone of its old buildings is in an entirely different mood from the glowing brick and sandstone of old Sydney.

Sydney has neither elegance nor calm, but Melbourne manages to have both, thanks to its parks and river, and its great avenues, which in a European city would be called boulevards. The artist Sidney Nolan, whose father was a tram driver and therefore had a good view of such things, says he was brought up to think that St. Kilda Road was the most beautiful street in the world. It may well be, despite the monstrous War Memorial Shrine that epitomizes all that was worst in Australian taste of the 1930's.

Sir Roy Grounds' new Art Gallery perhaps represents the same for the 1960's, an age when concepts were more important than people. The facade, grim as a Florentine palazzo, does not open to

Urban discord . . . Perth.

. . . Sydney.

reveal a lifting of the spirit as in Florence. Even on the outside there is a kind of a moat which repels everything except rubbish. One day the moat drew crowds; two ducks had waddled across St. Kilda Road, and were swimming happily, delighting people with the ease with which they shattered the severity.

The gold rush that made 'Marvellous Melbourne' rich also gave it a conscience. The Eureka Stockade, the gold miners' protest against government interference, was Australia's only armed uprising. It was important both as symbol and as fact; the enormous influx of population and wealth following the gold rush created two contradictory strains in the character of Victorians. On the one hand, they became Australia's most sturdy and aggressive radicals. On the other, they became Australia's greatest experts in the making and managing of money. Both strains were united in an allegiance to a 19th-century morality, and took note of the moral tale available in the collapse of the great property boom towards the end of the century.

Though the 1890's boom may have burst, Melbourne is still the financial capital of Australia, and money's greed for huge buildings has ruined Collins Street, which was once so beautiful. The biggest and most monstrous building, Collins Place, even half turns its buttocks to the once graceful street.

The new Collins Street is a monument to money. Yet there are really no rich people in Australia by American or European, let alone Middle Eastern, standards, although nothing else in Australia gives such a resolute impression of wealth as the Melbourne suburb of Toorak.

Conservative Melbourne used to be very British, and although Sir Robert Menzies, Australia's most enduring Prime Minister, was a country boy, he soon became a true Melbourne man, combining a respect for big business and the law with a personal ruthlessness and a genuine homage to the intellect, if not the *avant-garde*. Menzies did an enormous amount for education in Australia, but he and his friends were never happy with education that led to radical views. The old British conservatism of Collins Street and Sir Robert Menzies was not at all the same thing as the very subtle and Australian conservatism of Sandy Stone and Dame Edna

Everage, the most enduring of satirist Barry Humphries' characters, who draw their strength from the suburban bonds they share with their audience.

Nor is it the same as the multi-optioned conservatism of those who run things nowadays in Melbourne (which often means, in Australia as well). The old British conservatism of Sir Robert Menzies has given way to a much more dynamic, and Australian, conservatism. There are obvious manifestations, such as the fact that a Hungarian migrant, Arvi Parbo, is at the head of one of Australia's largest companies, Western Mining. But the new bosses like Sir Roderick Carnegie and Andrew Grimwade are much younger and more flexible in their thinking than their earlier counterparts. They are unmistakably Australian, not British, as much aware of Europe, China, the USA, Singapore or Hong Kong as they are of Britain. The same is true of their opposite numbers in the Trade Unions. The most brilliant and constructive Trade Union leader in Australia, Bob Hawke, is a passionate supporter of Israel. One of the most abrasive Unionists on the far left, Bill Hartley, is a supporter of the PLO.

Melbourne has been a most fertile breeding ground for scientists, particularly those associated with the Commonwealth Scientific and Industrial Research Organization and the Walter and Eliza Hall Institute of Medical Research. They have been highly radical and experimental in their work, but politically and socially conservative.

With the Victorian seriousness has gone a Victorian concern for liberty and the arts and sciences, although it is hard to say which is the greater miracle, the Opera House emerging from old style Labor Sydney, or the Victorian Arts Centre being sanctioned by that sturdy, culturally impervious, former Liberal Premier Sir Henry Bolte.

The Hamer government, with Eric Westbrook at the Ministry of the Arts, has made formidable achievements in the arts, from establishing the Tapestry Workshops to commissioning a number of artists, notably Mirka Mora, to paint the exterior of some of Melbourne's trams.

The arts have not always been so well received in Melbourne.

The Australian impressionist painters, Roberts, McCubbin, Streeton, Conder and others, had their open air painting camps at Box Hill and Heidelberg, and held their first exhibition, of paintings on nine-by-five inch cedar cigar box lids, at Buxton's Gallery in Swanston Street on 17th August, 1889. It was to be the most famous exhibition of local painting in the history of Australian art. The Art Critic of the *Argus* dismissed it as 'too ephemeral for consideration'.

The first great exhibition of modern art was brought to Australia by the *Melbourne Herald* in 1939, assembled by its art critic, Basil Burdett. The exhibition comprised 215 works by most of the modern masters since Gauguin and Cézanne, and had a profound effect on Australian painters, who had never seen original works of modern art. I saw it as a schoolboy and was amazed, baffled, excited and rapturous. But, like everybody else in Melbourne, I had to see it in the Town Hall, since the Director of the National Gallery of Victoria refused to have such an exhibition of degenerate daubs in the Gallery. As with the *Argus* critic of the nine-by-five inch show, the conflict was typical of Melbourne, which breeds a powerful conservative strain. There was an added drama in the case of the *Herald* exhibition, because the Chairman of the National Gallery Trustees was Sir Keith Murdoch (father of Rupert), who owned the *Herald*, which was sponsoring the exhibition.

By 1944, when I was there as a pilot in the RAAF, Melbourne was full of young, unknown artists with names like Sidney Nolan, Arthur Boyd, John Perceval and Albert Tucker. Their paintings were first illustrated and discussed in *Angry Penguins*, a literary magazine brought to Melbourne from Adelaide by Max Harris.

I remember Sid Nolan taking me around the Contemporary Art exhibition, pointing out in his gentle, courteous way what he thought were the best pictures and explaining why. It seemed to me that the truth of those brutal, desperate times had been found by those Melbourne artists, as by no one else in Australia. It was not that there were any paintings of actual war. Albert Tucker's *Images of Modern Evil* were all unmistakably set in Melbourne. The

Sail and steam: Opera House Sydney.

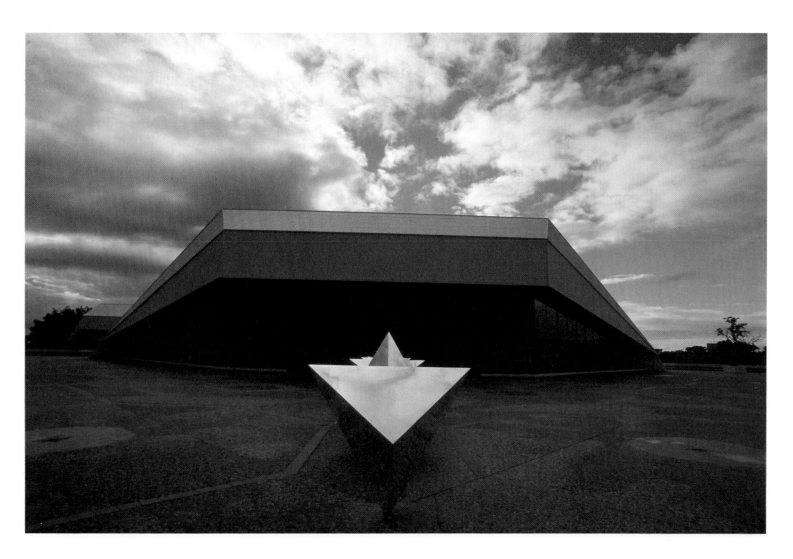

Stainless steel sculpture, Adelaide Festival Theatre.

artists were subtly in touch with those disjointed times.

Yet Melbourne even in wartime had the extraordinary ability during Cup Week to infect the whole of Australia with its abandon. On the first Tuesday in November, then and now, even Sydney gives itself over to stately, grey Melbourne. Moral Adelaide stops; the big North Terrace stores are deserted; in the chaste surroundings of the State Library no one is looking at a book; staff and readers are gazing at a TV set hung from the ceiling. It is the same all over Australia. Church schools have a raffle on the Cup; the radio commands the silence of every pub drinker in Australia; everything is hushed by that incredible chant of the race commentator, somewhere between a sung Eucharist and an orgasm. The horse in Australia has survived all the onslaughts of a mechanical age; surely few other countries in the world have a set of five postage stamps, each with a famous horse on it.

But the Melbourne Cup is more than horses. It is a culmination in Melbourne of a whole week that is an astonishing anomaly, a Victorian Mardi Gras. Melbourne is the money capital of Australia, but on Melbourne Cup day money is for luck and joy.

My first Melbourne Cup was in 1944. We were driving towards Flemington in an immense queue of cars (despite wartime rationing) in an old open Bentley, my wife the only girl amongst four RAAF pilots squeezed into the narrow seats. I wasn't too sure of the road so at a traffic light I asked the chauffeur of a Rolls Royce whether he was going to Flemington. Before he could reply, an old lady, wearing the Cup's top weight in hat and jewellery, leant out the back window and called out *Follow me boys*. So we did, and she led us into the Members' Stand, and after the race was over, even though the horse she was backing had only run second, she took all five of us to dinner at Menzies. That is the spirit of the Melbourne Cup, and it has not changed.

* * * *

An exasperated early English visitor called South Australia *a puffing Province*, and Adelaide has always been conscious, and rightly so, of its virtues. Its geographical advantages are obvious enough: the sea on one side, the hills on the other, and a Mediterranean climate, so fresh and sparkling that it is a shock to hear the radio announcer talking about the day's air pollution potential Alert.

The old Adelaide Hills gardens are classic examples of hating Australia; amidst the rhododendrons and cypresses and sycamores not a gum tree nor wildflower remains. Yet Adelaide has an incomparable advantage in the hundreds of acres of National Park in the hills. For nine months, recently, we were living in the hills, and each evening I used to walk the dogs along the trails cut to help fire fighters in the case of bush fire. All through those nine months there were wildflowers, changing from the reds of erica to the yellow of wattle, then to the purple and pink of the tethratheca, then to the gold and green and blue orchids, and finally the brilliant blue of billy-buttons and huge harebells with golden centres in their five pointed stars and stems so delicate they seem to be flowering in air. Even the grasses are as beautiful as flowers, especially the shivery grass with its nodding green-gold lanterns that are like the bodies of bees. In all those months of walking through wildflowers I never saw another human being, only black cockatoos with their squeaky-hinge cry and their slow black flap over the sombre trees, and a woodpecker striking his tiny anvil that echoed through the whole deep valley. All this was only 10 miles away from a city of three quarters of a million. I was delighted to have it to myself, but I often wondered why no one else was there. Were all those people watching TV?

Adelaide is the capital of the only State in Australia founded not for the benefit of England's convicts, but on democratic principles. When I was a boy in the 1920's and '30's Adelaide was devout, wowserish and true-blue British; however, this was not always so, and it is not so now. The city was planned and laid out by Colonel William Light, who was not a British Colonel at all, though he had been a gallant officer under Wellington in the Peninsular War. He had been a Lieutenant Colonel in a Spanish revolutionary army. He was also an illegitimate, English-Malay half-caste. In the Adelaide Town Hall every year staunch upholders of the British tradition toast the founder in Colonial Wine, seemingly unaware of his birth and poetic character. Certainly they and everyone else in Adelaide is aware of his plan, so far ahead of its time, with its wide streets, city squares and surrounding parklands.

Light had the temperament of a poet and an artist, and he would have approved of Adelaide's biennial Festival of Arts. At its heart is the Festival Centre, one of the finest theatre complexes in the world.

After New Zealand, South Australia was the first State in the world to give votes to women. It produced reforms like the Torrens Land Act, which simplified land titles and was copied around the world. There was a multitude of other achievements in social legislation. There was no gap between country and town in South Australia and there was no hostility between squatters and farmers because land sales were controlled from the beginning.

The radical tradition of Adelaide's founders ran to the end of the 19th century. But by the 1920's and '30's Adelaide was no more than a provincial country town that had settled into staid conservative ways, albeit enlivened by the best breed of eccentrics in Australia. There was an almost English style of gentry. In the early 1930's a car load of young bloods drove down North Terrace in an open car shooting out the street lights with a 12-bore. The policeman who stopped them did his best to disguise what he thought was a merry jest. No fuss was made, and of course everything was paid for.

The perfect image of conservative, British Adelaide is to me the sight of an elderly gentleman, in a heatwave of 105 degrees slowly crossing North Terrace from Government House to the Adelaide Club, wearing a tweed suit complete with waistcoat.

The tradition still continues. In December 1978 my daughter noticed an old gentleman of military bearing and moustache, in a suit of the best English tweed, walking from Rundle Mall towards a busker with a recorder, who had just finished playing an Irish jig. In a voice as impeccably grey as his suit he said to the bearded busker, *Do you think you could play Rule Britannia?*

Certainly, sir. The busker obliged, and threw in *The British Grenadiers* for good measure. The old gentleman thanked him, put

Parliament suspended, Canberra.

Parliament at rest, Melbourne.

$2 among the coins in his hat, and continued on his way.

Yet Tom Playford, who was Premier for longer than anyone else in British history except Walpole, was not a Conservative, and never a member of the Adelaide Club. The Adelaide establishment referred to Playford as a damned Red after he took over the Electric Supply Company for the State in the course of his heroic industrialization of South Australia.

To know a place well you should spend your childhood there, and then come back to it again after an absence of some years. Although a country boy, I had been brought to Adelaide often as a child, and I lived there when I went to the University and for a while at the end of the war. After six years in Europe, my wife and I returned to Adelaide in 1951.

Whether one was going for supper after the theatre, for drinks or for a quick visit to the lavatories, the focus was always the old South Australian Hotel with its cast iron veranda facing Parliament House. It was run by a formidable old lady, Mrs. O'Brien, who sat in the hall just inside the front door and never missed a face. It has long since been demolished, to make way for the Gateway Hotel and the Ansett Office.

In the early 1930's there were still stags' heads and leather chairs in the lounge, and a regular supply of mice to be chased. The dining room was ruled over by a head waiter, Lewy, whose strictness about dress once led him to order the Queen's dressmaker, Norman Hartnell, who was wearing an exquisite cravat, out of the dining room for not wearing a tie. After this incident a group of university students, wearing dinner jackets and black ties above, but nothing below except their underpants, paraded into the dining room holding a banner headed *Phooey to Lewy*.

A proprietory conservatism was enforced at all levels. During the '30's and '40's the Professor of English at the University was a notable Oxford scholar and wit, J.I.M. Stewart, who wrote detective stories under the name of Michael Innes. One of the key figures in Adelaide's Establishment, an architect, was reading Innes' latest novel and discovered to his horror that the butler in the book bore his name. The architect protested to the Vice-

Chancellor, Sir William Mitchell, and even to the Council. One day he met Professor Stewart in North Terrace and said to him *Nobody with my name ever accepted a menial position, and what is more, we once had a gardener called Stewart.*

An English visitor once remarked that the Adelaide Club was the finest 19th-century club in the world. Some of its members, visiting England in the 1950's and 1960's, found that the Old Country was showing regrettable signs of slipping into the 20th century. I recall one of them talking about his visit to Cambridge, where he discovered that the Captain of the cricket team was a Singhalese: *It wouldn't have happened in my day.* He continued, *I went to Oxford to see the golf and an Australian had the effrontery to introduce me to some dark fellow who was actually in the team. Golf! In my day there were a few of them about, mostly at Balliol, but of course nobody met them.*

In 1959, Rupert Max Stuart, a black Australian convicted of murder, divided Adelaide as it has never been before, and was not to be again until the Vietnam war. The editor of the evening *News*, Rohan Rivett, was the son of Sir David Rivett of CSIRO, and grandson of a radical parson who died on a rostrum in the Sydney Domain, defending an anti-Nazi. Rivett published material on Stuart's trial that led to his being brought to Court on a charge of criminal libel against the Chief Justice, Sir Mellis Napier. Ironically enough, he was defended by John Bray, who later became Chief Justice. It was a test case for the Establishment, which was determined to crush this unruly fellow from Melbourne with his championship of a black murderer. I recall Rohan having lunch with me at the time, looking haggard, laughing too loudly, breaking off in the middle of his sentences, confidently expecting to be in jail within six months. I was lecturing at the University at the time, and my students were busy organising protest marches through the city (this was before the era when students' marches became *de rigueur*).

In the end Rivett was acquitted, and shortly afterwards Rupert Murdoch, the owner of the paper, gave him a golden handshake and he went to Zurich to be President of the International Press Association.

In some ways the Stuart case marked the end of the Establishment's ascendancy in Adelaide. In the next 20 years Adelaide reverted to its original reforming, mild radicalism. Don Dunstan, who after an interval succeeded Playford, infuriated the extreme Left and the extreme Right exactly as Playford did. Playford, a Liberal, industrialized South Australia as a Labor leader might have been expected to do. Dunstan fought for South Australians' individual rights and access to the arts, as old-fashioned Australian Labor would never have done. People in one Australian State do not usually take much interest in other States; they tend to think of the nation as a whole. Yet I have been constantly surprised at the number of people in other States who have respected the stability and style Don Dunstan gave South Australia (which after all, in material resources, is the poorest of the States). A taxi driver in Sydney, hearing you were from Adelaide, would say: *How's that young Don of yours,* seemingly unaware that the Premier was in his 50's.

Dunstan's abrupt decision, in 1979, to resign from politics, forms an obvious demarcation line from which to look back on what he did, and failed to do, for South Australia. Most attractively, he gave not only South Australians but all Australians an idea that political leadership need not be humdrum party politics, that it could have a style and elegance which could reflect back into the capacity of ordinary people to enjoy life in Australia. When he wore pink shorts to Parliament House he was not being 'trendy', but accepting the reality of the Adelaide summer heat, and demonstrating that public life need not make people pompous (a most unusual proposition in Australia). Dunstan, like Sir Thomas Playford, was acutely aware of South Australia's limited natural resources and distances from markets. His establishment of the South Australian Film Corporation, which had a profound impact on the reawakening of the Australian film industry, and was soon to be imitated by other states, was typical of his attempts to give brains and imagination, which do not rely on geography, the opportunity to operate from South Australian soil. Under Dunstan's rule South Australia was also outstanding in the fields of education, consumer protection and the defence of citizens' rights. Some reforms or concepts, such as

Cities by the sea . . . Perth.

. . . Sydney.

those to do with homosexuality or abortion, or the establishment of the South Australian Festival Centre complex of theatres, were not originated by Dunstan, but might never have come to fruition without his enthusiasm.

Dunstan's weakness, like Whitlam's, was his failure to make contact with country people. This is ironical in that Dunstan has been the city man *par excellence*, just when city Australians began to be more aware of the country. One of his forbears went bust on a mean northern farm, and that may have helped to augment his suspicion of the country.

Dunstan's bad luck was that the downturn in Australia's economy has meant that South Australia's natural poverty, and for many years its near-isolation as a Labor state under a Federal Liberal coalition, has made it more than ever vulnerable to economic pressures. Dunstan was a great fighter for South Australia, but he did not always have much ammunition to fight with.

* * * *

Brisbane began badly, as the Moreton Bay of which the anonymous convict lamented:

To Moreton Bay I've found no equal
For excessive tyranny each day prevails.

Moreton Bay was only an outer convict settlement; it never had the initial status of Sydney or Hobart.

The city grew by accident around the muddy Brisbane river, and in a contemptuous way the river floods the city from time to time. Brisbane is the only old Australian city that has no beaches at its door; given the Australian passion for the sea, this makes the city a bit like a desperate creature throwing out its arms, one pointing North to Maroochydore, the other South to Surfer's Paradise.

Brisbane suffers from a lack of unique importance as a capital; no other Australian State capital has had to undergo such competition. Not only is Brisbane just over the border from New South Wales, but the State's shape and size, and its population distribution, make it topheavy. All along its enormous coastline is city after city – Rockhampton, Townsville, Cairns – each the centre for its region, not to mention inland cities such as Toowoomba or Mount Isa. The *laissez-faire* of Queensland politics reflects the lack of central focus in the State; every man might as well do his own thing, as Brisbane is too far away to know what he really needs.

For the rest of Australia, Brisbane is not much more than an airport en route to holidays or retirement on the Queensland coast. The lingering visitor sees the old style houses on stilts and immediately feels different: he is in the tropics. But Brisbane has far more to it than that. I find it symbolic that the man it was named after, Governor Brisbane, was not just a soldier, and a relatively enlightened Governor, but an astronomer who established the first observatory in Australia and was a fellow of the Royal Society and a D.C.L. of Oxford University. After Brisbane became a penal settlement in 1826, the old observatory was converted to a treadmill upon which convicts were condemned to trudge for up to 14 hours a day. Brisbane's oldest song runs:

Billy is a good boy now,
Billy is a good boy now,
They keep him still in the old treadmill,
Yes Billy is a good boy now.

There is also a nice Brisbane paradox in the activities of Dr. John Dunmore Lang, the first Presbyterian Minister in Australia, who on several return trips to Britain was so appalled by social conditions there that, without any authority, he arranged for three ships carrying about 600 immigrants to go to Moreton Bay. He was also instrumental in bringing out a number of German settlers. This splendidly energetic man was also a fiery Republican. By contrast, 130 years later, the regime of Johannes Bjelke-Petersen has passed special legislation under which, if the Commonwealth became a Republic, Queensland would not accept Republican status unless it passed a separate referendum.

The Queensland Premier's toughness and obliviousness to criticism have given Queensland a reputation in the south that provokes both fear and admiration. On the one hand prejudice, racial intolerance and self-interest with a sauce of religion; on the other an apparent return to the old individual values, and a whole-hearted acceptance of the benefits of the climate and of capitalism.

The writer David Malouf once suggested to me that no one could understand Queensland politics without realizing that most successful Queensland politicians are country people who left school at an early age. Queensland's geography, its vast interior and its big towns far apart on an extended coastline, has imposed severe educational difficulties on Queenslanders. Although some excellent boarding schools were early established away from Brisbane, at Toowoomba or Charters Towers, it was very difficult for most Queenslanders, until recent years, to acquire any higher education. Joh's cabinet is mostly composed of people who suffered from this handicap. Of course, in the rough-house of Australian politics this is, pragmatically, not necessarily a handicap at all. One of the most successful politicians in Australia's history, South Australia's Sir Thomas Playford, used to say with relish that he was educated in the University of Hard Knocks.

In Queensland itself, people at all levels of society are strangely ambivalent about Joh. Their attitudes were nicely caught by a Brisbane taxi driver to whom I innocently said, *And what's Joh been up to lately?*

Listen, mate, he replied, *we can call Joh a bloody peanut if we want to, but don't you buggers from down South try it on.*

The rest of Australia either sees Brisbane clouded by the repressive anti-Civil Rights legislation of Joh Bjelke-Petersen or applauds Joh's uncompromising championship of old extreme right-wing values. To my mind, those who admire Joh for his toughness do so at the eventual cost of their own liberties.

Architecturally, Brisbane has not much of a heritage, but it is accumulating some fine new buildings and beginning the construction of a cultural complex by the river near Victoria Bridge. Robin Gibson, the architect, can observe what is good or

Multi-national sausages, Melbourne market.

'Fish real cheap today!' Adelaide market.

bad in Roy Grounds' design in Melbourne and Colin Hassell's in Adelaide. But whatever he does he has a chance of achieving some sort of centre for Brisbane which will be cultural in more than name.

Brisbane has known hard times; during the Second World War it was like an occupied city, with the Americans commandeering everything, especially the girls. I remember walking into Lennon's Hotel in my uniform, a flight lieutenant pilot in the RAAF, and being told to clear out as I was not an American. Brisbane retains some of the engaging raffish quality it had those days. Brothels were legal, and I was amused after the war to find that an old sergeant pilot friend of mine had married a rich widow who was in fact the madam of the biggest brothel in Brisbane. When he died, every whore in Brisbane was at his funeral.

Unexpectedly, Brisbane, and Queensland, have spent more money on the arts than New South Wales. Though its writers flee, it keeps on producing more. Judith Wright, who came from New England, lived for many years in Queensland; Tom Shapcott, David Malouf, Rodney Hall, Murray Bail, and many others are all Queenslanders. For years Brian Jonstone ran one of Australia's most successful art galleries in Brisbane and there are a number of good private galleries now, even though the State Gallery, at last rebuilding, has been a disgrace.

Despite the emigration, the novelist Xavier Herbert remains in Cairns, and there have been some sturdy migrants to Brisbane and Queensland, such as the poet and musician John Manifold, the artist Lawrence Daws, and Bruce Dawe, who is teaching at Toowoomba.

Brisbane's greatest asset is its extraordinarily good-natured and hospitable inhabitants. It also has a number of delicious pleasures such as its tropical fruits and gardens; the enormous mud crabs at Baxters or Burleigh Marrs; and the Moreton Bay Bugs, which are like little crayfish tails with legs, and are succulent if absolutely fresh, and dry as hessian if stale.

Brisbane's tropical flowers, admirable and full of colour though they are, give an anonymous quality, for the tropics overpower nationality. Poincianas come from Madagascar, poinsettias from

Central America, bougainvilleas from South America, jacarandas from the West Indies. To be unkind, one could add that Surfer's Paradise comes from Miami.

* * * *

Perth has light as sparkling as Adelaide's, and the estuary of the Swan River opens up the centre of the city. But the wildflowers in King's Park, Perth, and the native flowers in Perth's gardens, are like nothing in Australia or anywhere else.

Perth is a sort of symbol of Western Australia. Like a stage set, it has a great, rich front. But if you walk just one street up from St. George's Terrace you are into a country town. In the same way the rim of civilization round the sea disguises the gigantic emptiness of the biggest of Australian States.

One should go many times to Perth, by sea, land and air, to be aware how precarious its bold front is. The first time I went to Perth, in 1938, was an endless slog across the Nullarbor Plain in a dusty train. The last time was in a jet from Adelaide which, even for a jet, takes a long time. In between I have been across the Great Australian Bight in a cargo steamer, the huge swells burying the bow and forward hatches back to the bridge; I have flown in my sister's little Cessna below the 600-foot cliffs at the edge of the Nullarbor, one of the wonders of the world; and I have driven with my wife on the old gravel road, and camped the night in the abandoned Eucla telegraph station (which is now covered in sand) in a waking dream of ghosts.

In the old days of sea travel, Perth's port of Fremantle, with its lovely old golden stone buildings amidst the galvanized iron, was your last sight of Australia going, and your first coming back.

Returning to Perth in 1951, after five years in the black and bombed cities of Europe, it was as if the front door were permanently open, as I was exposed again to the light and openness of Australia. I wrote at the time: *We were lucky, we had landed in Western Australia, whose inhabitants are the kindest and most courteous of all Australians, and whose wildflowers are incomparable; even our grumpy taxi driver wanted to show them to us. He drove us through King's Park, that astonishing area of virgin scrub in the midst of a city, through the shaggy, down-hanging, grey-green scrub, past the startling red iridescent green of the kangaroo paws, weirdest of wildflowers, around the Swan River to the geometrical town. When we walked through the park on the next day a magpie sang for half an hour on the same branch of the same tree, and this was unmistakably home, the far blue light surpassing even that of Greece in clarity, the spacious quiet, the brown colours and the long, low contours. Memory lies within us like wine in a bottle, and deepest are the dregs, no matter whether ugly or useless, odd things like the way a man rolls his cigarette, a certain brand of petrol, the shape of the veranda of a one storied house, a monkey-puzzle pine, the colour of the brown paint on the post of a shop. In a hotel I was surprised to hear a man mention the words 'Greek vase', but reassured when he continued: 'Yeah. He came in seven to one in the third race.' I felt unmistakably at home.*

If you went to the Art Gallery in the early '50's you would find the assistants sitting out in the sun, braces over grey shirts and blue serge trousers pulled up to the knees. Inside the front door was a replica of the Venus de Milo with a plug in her navel to which was attached a large notice, *No Smoking*. Now Perth has recently completed a new art gallery that will have almost as much space as Sydney's.

Since the aeroplane took over from the ship, Perth is no longer the gateway to Australia. In its isolation it has become something quite different. The sealing of the infamous dusty old road from Adelaide has given Perth a new attraction to the mobile Australian. In 1978 about 200,000 visitors drove across the Nullarbor. At the same time, given packaged air tours, Perth residents turn their backs on Australia, for it is cheaper to go for a holiday in the Philippines, Indonesia, Singapore or even Mauritius than to go to Sydney. This is all part of an acceptance of Asia by Australians, the effects of which no one as yet can measure.

Perth, even now, has some of the hectic independence of a mining town, even though it is hundreds of miles away from the great mines. A skyscraper like Hamersley House looks solid

Cool streetscape in a hot town. Quorn, northern South Australia.

Well-dressed pub, central Melbourne.

enough, but what if no one wants all that iron ore? On the other hand, somebody has just discovered diamonds. The nickel of Poseidon is a bad memory, but gold is still as rich as gold; 80 years after Kalgoorlie and Coolgardie, there are successful goldfields operating today.

We were talking to a Perth businessman who recalled sitting as a child on a kangaroo skin rug listening to his old uncle tell him how he and his mate found the first gold at Coolgardie. They all jumped up and down yelling for joy, and then they filled their pockets and shirtsleeves with ore and went to make their claim. But when they got back the area was already pegged. So the uncle went into transport, supplying the goldfields, and made a fortune, unlike most miners.

The fortunes in Perth nowadays have been made by mining entrepreneurs, people like Lang Hancock and Alan Bond.

Perth's main industries, the Kwinana oil refinery, the BHP steel mills, the Alcoa Alumina refinery and the huge naval base are all concentrated around Garden Island and Cockburn Sound. The consequent onslaught on the Sound's ecology, the salinisation of land, especially in the South-West with its diminishing forests, and the shortage of water in Perth itself have forced the *laissez-faire* Government to launch some enquiries.

I asked Hancock a few years ago to contribute a chapter to a symposium I was editing called *Republican Australia?* He sent me a piece which urged Western Australian secession, and ended with a Bjelke-Petersen-like plea for Western Australia to stay attached to the Queen, whatever the rest of Australia did.

Sir Charles Court, the Premier, does not believe in secession, but he is almost as conservative as Hancock, which is something very different from the flexible conservatism of Melbourne. Whether Labor or Liberal has been in office, Western Australian politics have always been conservative. This conservatism also manifests itself as a stabilizing force in more radical areas; it is interesting that the most important union leader and the most influential administrator of post World War II Australia, R.G. Hawke and Dr. H.C. Coombs, both grew up in Western Australia, although Hawke was born in South Australia.

That thin rim of settlement makes Western Australians particularly responsive to the sea, even by Australian standards.

As a schoolboy on my first visit to Perth in 1938 I was taken to North Cottlesloe beach. On that beautiful December day, there was such an ease and lack of pressure amongst the kindly, carefree people sunbaking on the glorious beach, I could not imagine anyone in Perth working. In 1938 I could never have foreseen that 40 years later, not a mile to the north, on Swanbourne beach, there would be thousands of people in the water and on the sand wearing no clothes at all. This sensible hedonism is what makes conservative Perth so attractive.

More and more people today are going to Fremantle, particularly for its Art Centre, a genuine community affair taking in all the arts at every level. The Art Centre is affiliated with a publishing press and an art gallery, and a programme called Arts Access, through which the Centre sends out weavers and potters to all over the vast State, from Albany to Wyndham.

It is nicely ironic that the lovely old limestone walls of the Fremantle Art Centre were built by convicts to house 'lunatics'. It is odd that lunatics, as they were called in the 19th century, despised and misunderstood as they were, had some of the finest buildings in Australia erected for them. The most handsome of all is at Glenside, in South Australia, built in the 1870's. Such grand buildings for the disadvantaged are scattered all over Australia. One surprised and slightly indignant English visitor to the Bendigo Benevolent Home in 1860 wrote: *Here you lodge the recipients of public charity in just such mansions as the estated gentry in Great Britain are in the habit of erecting for their private residences.*

Perth has had its writers and artists, but their context is not specific to the city. Robert Juniper is the most hedonistic of painters, but his lyrics of praise are of the goodness of nature. Katharine Susannah Prichard wrote of the gold mines, the timber country and the station country; apart from Xavier Herbert's books, her *Coonardoo* is still the finest Australian novel of black and white. Mary Durack writes about her ancestors in the North-West, Randolph Stow about his in Geraldton and further afield, Fay Zwicky composes a Kaddish for her father. Nicholas Hasluck's novel *Quarantine* is set in Suez in the 1930's, although his new novel *The Blue Guitar* is about people in Perth. There have been a number of good Perth historians, Nicholas' mother Alexandra and his father Paul Hasluck, but in art as well as life Perth is a gateway; artists and writers look through it rather than at it.

* * * *

When you walk around Hobart, you find that Mount Wellington, the Derwent and the shape of the harbour tend to make the city an enclosure, almost a sanctuary, an island within an island. Considering Hobart's size, a remarkable number of fine writers, in particular, have either come from it or been attracted to it: James McAuley, Gwen Harwood, Vivian Smith, Hal Porter and others. A.D. Hope is a sort of refugee from Tasmania. So, I suppose, on rather a different level, was Errol Flynn.

Though Hobart can be hot and certainly hedonistic, a clear cold seems closer to the norm, as in Vivian Smith's poem:

Winter is the heart of praise.
In praise of clarity the winds blow
from the cold South across the hills
and shake the pear tree free of snow —

Convict wrongs hang over beautiful 18th-century Hobart, as they do over Sydney, shadowed by the genocide of the black Tasmanians. It is fashionable, and self-indulgent, to pretend to feel a personal guilt; but anyone looking at the paintings and drawings of Petit, Duterrau, Bock and Dowling cannot help feeling haunted. What is especially macabre is that the ghosts, as in Dante's *Inferno*, strike each other down. Some of the worst offences against the Tasmanian Aborigines were committed by convict shepherds, and their atrocities provoked the blacks into attacking the stations. The settlers, alas, retaliated with relish. The crimes of the British Tasmanians against the blacks are rendered more terrible by the evidence, especially from the French explorers, who predated the British, that the blacks were a friendly, humorous and dignified people, highly strung and nervous by nature. They never fought any war against the whites, though that was the excuse given for their extermination.

It would be sentimental nonsense to say that the atrocities of British settlers 120 years ago cast a pall over one's enjoyment of Hobart. It's rather that the past gives a depth, a quality of poetry. Also the Georgian architecture of Hobart, as of the great country houses such as Panshanger, reaches back beyond the history and appearance of most of the rest of Australia, which begins with the Victorian era. This presence is strong in Tasmania, distancing it on yet another level from the mainland of Australia.

The best way to see Hobart, which is scarcely available now, is from the pilot's seat in a Tiger Moth bi-plane, preferably at night. During the war I was a Flying Instructor at Western Junction, near Launceston, and we used to take turns going down to Hobart for a glorious lazy fortnight of co-operation with the Army, particularly their anti-aircraft and searchlight crews. All you had to do was fly up and down the Derwent, every now and then taking some evasive action, which could be quite sensational at night. The searchlight operators, who lacked radar or any homing devices, were extremely inefficient. The white fingers of their lights would probe the darkness anywhere except where it hid the little yellow aircraft chugging along at a mere 70 m.p.h.

The half-darkened city lay on either side of the black strip that was the Derwent, and you were uneasily conscious of the presence of dark Mount Wellington waiting to destroy you if you turned the wrong way. Every now and then you would feel sorry for the wretched anti-aircraft troops, and attempt to dive into their searchlight beams to give them a chance. But just as you were about to reach a beam it would wander drunkenly off into the further darkness.

You were your own boss, and thus, if some more tempting proposition offered, or if a hangover were too severe, you could ring up the Army and tell them the weather looked a bit risky for flying, and retire to the luxury of the old pre-casino Wrest Point Hotel. The hotel curved right down into the harbour like a ship,

87

Alternatives, Melbourne.

Staples, Melbourne.

and one morning I was startled to awake and see a grey cliff outside the window. It was the *Queen Elizabeth*, on her way back from the Middle East.

If Adelaide and Perth were country towns in those days, Hobart was a village. I first arrived there by train, and when I went to get out of the carriage I found there was no platform. You just had to jump down and clump along through the mud, as if you were at a country siding. I was going to stay with a girlfriend, a gorgeous blonde who later became Miss Tasmania. She drove me to her house in Sandy Bay, where her parents treated me, an unknown sergeant pilot, as if I were a Wing Commander. After her father had given me a very satisfying Hobart Cascade beer, he asked me how I liked Hobart. *Oh it's lovely*, I answered, *but you do have a very primitive railway station. Look at my muddy shoes!*

Oh dear, interrupted my blushing girlfriend, *I didn't tell you. Daddy is Commissioner of Railways.*

Hobart has never lost a certain intimate quality. It is not only that it is small but the people know each other and take part in affairs. Social arrangements seem very old fashioned. When I returned to Hobart in 1962 the front page headline in *The Mercury* was *Four Barons at Government House*. The Government House presence is still very strong. A recent collection of poems in honour of the late James McAuley has a Preface by the Governor, Sir Stanley Burbury, K.C.V.O., K.B.E. This is something admirable in itself no doubt, but inconceivable in any other Australian State. At the end of his Preface Sir Stanley writes: *James McAuley was happy to live in Tasmania. We are proud that in our quiet, unhurried way of life, and in the beauties of our countryside, bush, and sea, he like many exponents of the 'sister arts' from early Colonial days found contentment and inspiration.*

The citizens of Hobart are certainly far removed from the description of them 140 years ago by one George Boyes, the Colonial Auditor: *The people in this Colony very much resemble the Americans in their presumption, arrogance, impudence and conceit.*

Yet gentle Hobart is in many ways still a part of that greater penal colony, universal suburbia. The Hobart poet Gwen Harwood has written the cruellest of all poems about suburbia.

She practices a fugue, though it can matter
to no one now if she plays well or not.
Beside her on the floor two children chatter,
then scream and fight. She hushes them. A pot
boils over. As she rushes to the stove
too late, a wave of nausea overpowers
subject and counter subject. Zest and love
drain out with soapy water as she scours
the crusted milk. Her veins ache. Once she played
for Rubinstein, who yawned. The children caper
round a sprung mousetrap where a mouse lies dead.
When the soft corpse won't move they seem afraid.
She comforts them; and wraps it in a paper
featuring: Tasty dishes from stale bread.

It is not only a poem about isolation, but about the lack of excellence. The pianist is caught between her knowledge of her own imperfection (*Rubinstein, who yawned*) and the ignorance of her neighbours (*it can matter to no one now if she plays well or not.*) And the housewife is lost between the seed of passion that produced her children and the soapy water and crusted milk that is her daily life.

Gwen Harwood is too fine a poet merely to be playing the game of attacking suburbia. For years Australian suburbia has been blasted by critics, especially academics, and it should long ago have withered away in shame. Partly it owes its immunity to the fact that its critics themselves have been so essentially suburban, happy to share its comforts and space.

What is alarming is that suburbia seems to destroy its own virtues. Even a small city like Hobart is not totally suburban.

* * * *

Canberra, comparable in population, is planned and doomed to be nothing but democratic suburbia in a freshly invaded countryside.

Of all Australia's cities, Canberra should be the most hopeful. After many vicissitudes under the unaesthetic hands of Government, the inner city was laid out according to the brilliant plan of Walter Burley Griffin. It is rich in parks and playing fields, contains a concentration of intelligent and responsible and affluent citizens, leavened (if that is the word) by politicians and diplomats, and flows into suburbs devoid of poverty or slums. Canberra ought to be a great place to live in. It would seem to have achieved all the ideals of the town planner. Which just goes to show how inadequate those ideals are.

For clear, curving Canberra is black and twisted with alcohol, drugs, vandalism and unhappy sex, and it is probably the most dangerous city in Australia for children to grow up in. There are several reasons for this disturbing paradox. The youthfulness of the city of Canberra is not good for the youth of Canberra. There is no variety, there are no shades of experience; there is nowhere to disappear to, nowhere to go. Canberra, so bureaucratized, makes a good case for Russian-style 'Palaces of Youth', centres where everything is available from ballet to musicmaking, drama groups to gymnastics. Despite all its schools, an extremely good University, and a college of Advanced Education, Canberra exists for the convenience of middle-aged people. Politicians, diplomats, civil servants and academics have everything provided for them, including each other's tightly graded parties. But outside the educational establishments there is nothing for the young, a hazard aggravated by the fact that both parents of so many Canberra families go to work outside the home. There are grim warnings here for the rest of Australia.

Another hazard is the impermanence of Canberra residents. Australians as a whole are great travellers but not great movers; anyone doubting this should live for a while in the U.S.A., where huge sections of the population are constantly moving. But in Canberra politicians symbolize the temporary occupancy of all those neat houses. Grandparents may visit, but they live somewhere else, for scarcely anyone has roots in Canberra. To compensate for this, large numbers of Canberra people are hobby farmers, made whole by horses or rotary hoes. Likewise, a remarkable number of Canberra people have tents, caravans or houses on the coast, to offset the fact that Canberra is the only Australian city not on the sea.

Two and a half million people a year, mostly Australians, visit Canberra; it is a sort of museum of modern artifacts, where the exhibits move, talk and sneeze. But there is no contact between visitor and exhibit. Australian politicians get out of touch and Australian bureaucrats get out of hand because there is no rough reality around them, no one to meet and cut them down to size. In London or Paris, government is in the midst of the people. Washington, of course, is isolated, but Government and administration in the U.S.A. are far less centralized than they are in Australia.

All in all, Canberra, so beautiful, so full of charming and intelligent people, so delightful to visit for a few days, is the greatest disaster to have been inflicted on the Australian people.

The poet David Campbell, who died in 1979, could remember watering a mob of sheep below City Hill near what is now the concrete and asphalt of Constitution Avenue. The sheep, the foxes, the hawks and hares have all gone, although they survive in Campbell's clear and beautiful poems. The light of Canberra is still clear and beautiful, but the city's presence has deeply disturbed the balance of nature, and most grievously, the nature of life in the whole of Australia.

Vintage roofing, Sydney.

Terrace house, Melbourne.

Suburbia

Who would want to live in Australian suburbia – satirized by Patrick White and Barry Humphries and David Williamson, castigated by Ronald Conway, insulted by Jonathan King, patronized by Max Harris, analysed by Robin Boyd, and understood by Phillip Adams? Yet most Australians are suburbanites. And when they go to the theatre and read the books and the newspaper columns, they laugh at themselves and go on putting in the next season's sweet peas. They are gardeners, and they do not mind being the compost heap of Australia, into which all the rubbish is thrown, as long as it is organic, and anything and everything grows from the soil they enrich.

Not only do most Australians live in the suburbs of the big cities, but the values and lives of those who live in country towns are also suburban. At the opposite corners of the continent, at Lake's Entrance, Karratha, Albany or Cairns, there are separate houses with gardens, cars, TV, maybe a boat, maybe a swimming pool, and a hidden mortgage.

The apparent monotony of this individual sprawl, and the pleasure it gives those who live there, arouses fury in many intellectuals. They denounce suburbia for its emptiness, its loneliness, its ugliness, its lack of soul (whilst mostly living in suburbia themselves). They see these suburban dwellers dumbly acquiescing in the screaming inanities of commercial radio, believing all the advertisements in the papers and on TV, gambling away the money that enslaves them, upholding conservatism in politics and materialism in life.

But what if it is not like that at all? How do you reconcile this mindless desert of suburbia with the fact that so many of Australia's great men and women came from the suburbs and comfortable country towns? It cannot all be rebellion, challenge and response. The suburbs produced Joan Sutherland, Sidney Nolan, Arthur Boyd, Gough Whitlam and Barry Humphries, as the country towns produced Norman Lindsay, R.G. Menzies, Macfarlane Burnett, Robert Helpmann, H.C. Coombs and R.J. Hawke. The exceptions are interesting. Patrick White, Russell Drysdale, Judith Wright, David Campbell, Mary Durack and Lord Casey came from the pastoral aristocracy; Lady Casey from a Collins Street doctor's house; Don Dunstan from Fiji; Tom Playford from a farm. The choice is arbitrary, the lists could be prolonged, but by far the majority of the men and women of talent or genius would be from those little separate houses with flowers in the front, vegetables at the back, seething with brains and soul and creative imagination.

A minor versifier of the 1930's, Bartlett Adamson, wrote about an inner suburb of Sydney:

I tell you it nearly makes me burst,
The things I think of in Darlinghurst.

The critics are successors to those who apologized for Australia's inferiority to Trollope in 1872 and to the English ballet critic Arnold Haskell 70 years later, prompting Haskell to write in his sympathetic study, *Waltzing Matilda*:

The intellectual doubter is a rabbit gradually undermining self-confidence and prestige.

By day the Australian suburbs are wide open. Lawns run to the edge of the footpath, and children, dogs and cats can be killed with ease by the passing car. Everything is on view, just like a supermarket. It is all so neat and tidy, and, inside the houses, safe. The car is the common bond, but there is no common meeting ground except the supermarket or the eating houses (they could not be called restaurants) where people are refuelled as hygienically and identically as cars, with the exception that the humans have been trained to dispose of their own rubbish. In these places the murals resemble those of a pre-school and the seats are like a merry-go-round, and all the children are given paper caps with the name of the eating-house on them. The choice is limited to burgers and bits of chicken. Oddly enough, the men who prepare the food wear hair-nets but the women do not. They are all behind chromium and glass; there are no waiters, nothing mingles except the piped music. You are handed a little tray, the only thing not digestible or disposable, and you find a seat with a cast-iron lace back made of plastic. On the toilet doors, centrally placed, are drawings and the words *Kings* and *Princesses*. (Presumably *Queens* might be subject to misunderstanding.)

A young woman with her own and her neighbours' little children sits at a separate table, her head in her hands except when one of the children is naughty or cries. There are no napkins, salt or pepper, knives, forks or spoons. A father, mother, and two children, all wearing their paper hats, swiftly ingest their burgers, and put their trays in the rack and their rubbish in the prim mouth of the bin that looks like the King's postbox. Everything is gleaming, freshly painted, and occasionally a woman dressed like a funfair attendant wanders around, in case some recalcitrant subject of the Burger King has not disposed of his rubbish.

The essence of one marketing concept of daytime suburbia — sanitized, safe, fit for the whole family and especially the kiddies — is distilled into such places. It is a sort of desert through which suburban dwellers have to fight until they reach the next real waterhole where there are weeds, tadpoles and animal droppings.

But by night the suburbs darken into mystery. Fly into a city at night and you see pools of blackness between the isolated street-lights and the golden rivers of the multi-lane highways. The drapes are drawn in the temples of TV, the streets are deserted. If you land, and drive out along the six-track highways, north out of Sydney, south out of Adelaide, west out of Melbourne, east out of Perth, there are the same landmarks, their lighthouses flashing the same signals: Happy Jack's, Pizza Bar, Kentucky Fried Chicken, Mac-Donalds. You could be in Dallas or Kansas City. At the drive-in movies the cars' eyes glint at the huge high screen where the violence and rape that are banned in safe suburbia are ritually enacted, real enough but never reaching out so far as to open the car door.

On the highways the cars stream by. But two distinct types prowl — one is the police; the other the GT black speed-striped V8 Falcons and Holdens, twin exhausts rumbling, the drivers all tiny men with wispy beards, alongside them identical girls devoid of animation (the radio supplies all that is needed of that).

In the smaller country towns the scene is a little different. The GT monsters suddenly do a drag burst down the main street, and race out on the main road for a few miles, then off on to a gravel road where they spray round in 180° slides known as youees, or, if skilful enough, right round the full 360°, and off again. Not to go anywhere.

Boats in everybody's back yard . . . Sydney.

In the swim of suburbia.

Henry Williams (who ironically was killed in a car accident in 1978) wrote a brilliant novel, *My Love Had A Black Speed-Stripe*, about the destructive obsessions behind those V8's with their mag wheels and their polished heads.

The destructive and pollutive aspects of the motor car need no comment, though it is worth while reflecting that those most hostile to the motor car are usually urban intellectuals who don't possess one. Henry Williams' black vision of obsession was relevant enough, but, of all people in the world, Australians probably enjoy cars the most. Perhaps it is also because they need them the most. It is simply incalculable what the car has meant to people who live in the country; it also, quite apart from poor public transport, means a great deal to those who live in the suburbs, for the bonds it gives them with the country and the sea. The cars themselves are symbolic of Australian society and tastes. There is multi-ethnic and prosperous and sophisticated Australia: BMW, Alfa Romeo, Mercedes, Volvo, Jaguar, Citroën and so on. And there is suburban Australia: Holden, Ford, Valiant and all the Japanese cars. But also in the suburbs are those who drive the multi-ethnic cars, perhaps not quite new, and the four-wheel drive Toyotas and Land-Rovers.

The Holden itself, which used to be called 'Australia's Own Car', is in itself a mini-social-history of Australia. The first Holden was almost forced on General Motors by Prime Minister Chifley; to the credit of both, it was launched in November 1948. It was a surplus design, unwanted by Detroit, thought good enough for simple Australia, and was as stark as a car could be in 1948; it had no heater, a vacuum-operated windscreen wiper that stopped when you accelerated, and a tendency to fly off the road unless you had two people in the back seat or a sandbag in the boot. But it was phenomenally reliable, and a model of modest and sensible specifications compared to the parent American dinosaurs, or to the later V8 models that succeeded it. Its 2.2-litre six-cylinder engine developed only 60 b.h.p., but gave it 35 m.p.g. and 80 m.p.h. It had a three-speed gearbox with no synchromesh on first, and upholstery of plastic that stuck to the buttocks and back in the Australian heat. It weighed just under a ton.

Thirty years later Holdens had a lot of comforts and were still reliable and were not as vulgar as American cars, but they totally lacked the character of the original model. Their chief competitors, Ford and Valiant, were equally overbodied and boring to drive. Then a revolution happened. General Motors-Holden launched the Commodore, a thoroughly Australianized version of the Opel ('Australia's Own German Car', one might say), which not only was a sensible size and shape but also, to the joy of all motoring critics, a delight to drive, a sophisticated European car completely suitable for Australian roads. A similar process has gone on at Ford, with the restyling of the Falcon. The enthusiasm with which these cars have been greeted is yet another proof that Australian suburbia has become more demanding, and is no longer prepared to put up with out-of-date concepts of its needs.

Like the international Commodore, there is, on the surface, nothing particularly Australian about the suburbs, except the shrubs and trees in the gardens. You could be in America. The rituals are the same. Some years ago when I was teaching at an American university one of my students, a particularly pretty girl, came to the class with her arm in a sling. She said to me, *My boyfriend leaned on me at the drive-in, and dislocated my shoulder.* Such dangers are international.

Eighty years ago Australians were already showing a strong preference for living in suburbs in separate houses. As for Australian society, Beatrice and Sidney Webb in 1898 found it *just a slice of Great Britain and differs only slightly from Glasgow, Manchester, Liverpool and the* suburbs *of London.*

Fifty years ago Sir Keith Hancock, then a young professor of history living in Adelaide, was writing in the London *New Statesman* how Australians had brought the country into the cities, where they lived *far withdrawn behind wooden fences and green hedges which enclose their gardens. The vast majority of country acres which have been brought into the cities have been parcelled out into innumerable little front-gardens and back-yards. To these the clerk and the retailer retire with spade and watering-can, to satisfy the primitive half-forgotten instincts of their villein and yeoman ancestry.* Hancock admitted that these houses *contain some of the comforts and all the decencies of life,* but he saw divisive influences at work. *The streets are suspicious and contemptuous of one another. There are basic-wage streets, there are 300 a year streets, there are 500, 700, 1,100 a year streets . . . Australian cities are marked out into zones of comparative comfort – comfort without taste . . . Yet even the clerk seems to have some dim realization of the dullness and monotony of Antipodean suburbia. Why else should he yearn for all those little fancies, audacities, and embellishments which will distinguish 'Edithville', his home, from 'Wywurrie', the home of his neighbour? . . . This vast suburban mass is inevitably opposed to subversive change . . . There is no fear of its pulling down the comfortable house which it inhabits.*

Hancock's tone is unmistakably that of the academic observer, though not even the most righteous today could speak quite in that way about *clerks* and *retailers.* Hancock himself was, but for the grace of God, suburban, for his father was an Anglican Archdeacon and he was born in Melbourne and raised in a country town.

Some of Hancock's observations are no longer true. The houses are no longer withdrawn; the fences are all down; everything is shared, except life itself. The strict economic gradations seem obvious, Collingwood to Toorak, Redfern to Darling Point, but what is not obvious is the mobility behind the apparent segregation. Nor is it true today that *the streets are suspicious and contemptuous of one another.* In fact, I doubt if it was true of Adelaide 50 years ago.

In an amusing poem, *Suburban Segregation,* Colin Thiele sees the sun rising on Adelaide, creeping down the *superior slopes* of Beaumont and Springfield to the coarser areas of Bowden and the Port.

A singlet-covered barrel-chest,
The Portside yawns to flex its strength;
Springfield awake
Powders and bathes at length.

Beaumont and Bowden know their place
By carriage-drives and dust-bin lids;
Mylady sniffs, and Bloggs avers
He wouldn't live up there for quids.

48/215 – *the first model Holden.*

A number of late model Holdens.

Bloggs' comment has the humour and the idiom that eludes the Jeremiahs from Hancock to Jonathan King. Both humour and idiom are desegregating agents, eloquent of a comfortable at-home feeling; they are equally possible in Beaumont or Bowden, but more likely in Bowden. It is gentility, intellectual snobbery and rancour that set people apart.

Of course, the essential pattern of suburbia keeps families together and houses apart. The trend to togetherness was brilliantly sent up some years ago in the satirical *Mavis Bramston* TV show. These bursts of togetherness do not last for long, and the separateness returns. *The Great Australian Loneliness* was the title Ernestine Hill used for a book about the Outback, but there are two Australian lonelinesses, and for some the worst is suburban. Bruce Dawe wrote in *Up The Wall*:

Spiel, like the horizon, closes in,
The talk-back oracle's suave
Palming a hidden menace, children carve
The mind up with the scalpels of their din.

She says, 'They nearly drove me up the wall!'
She says, 'I could have screamed, and then the phone —!'
She says, 'There's no one round here I can call
If something should go wrong. I'm so alone!'

'It's a quiet neighbourhood,' he tells his friends.
'Too quiet, almost!' They laugh. The matter ends.

Bruce Dawe has caught the true background to the suburban loneliness. The segregation is not of the suburban houses, but of the sexes. Everything has been built around family life, and that only exists at weekends. That is, if the man does not play golf or go fishing with his mates. During the week the suburbs of factory workers are more fortunate than those of executives, for the men (who aren't still in the pubs) come home and have their evening meal early with the children; whereas the executives, from choice or necessity, work back at the office and do not come home until the children are in bed.

Security, safety and comfort are the seals of suburbia. And why not? Who would want, for their lives, insecurity, danger and discomfort? Yet the dangers hint at excitement, through the papers and the TV. And there are those like Roy in Patrick White's play *The Season at Sarsaparilla* who scent blood and wonder about wars and revolutions, and whether they should *get involved in something*. So when Judy tells him she is beginning to see that life has *a fascinating regularity* he bursts out with *But it's just from that that we're trying to escape!*

The passions must have an outlet, and in the confines of suburbia the natural one would seem to be in the last line of Colin Thiele's poem: *Who, then, will sleep with whom tonight?* In fact, the distinctive Australian passion is for gambling. The suburban solitary vice is the tote, the lottery, the money games, the poker-machines (in New South Wales). For company, there is the racecourse and the football.

The old bushrangers demanded your money or your life. The one-armed bandit demands your money *and* your life. It is not only the amount of money surrendered to them, but the awful solitary concentration, especially on the faces of respectable middle-aged ladies, as if pulling down the handle of the machine and listening to the crash of coins were a revenge on all those lonely hours in kitchens and laundries, the rattle of cutlery in the stainless steel sink.

But the loneliness and the quiet are deceptive. They can disguise the hopes of Judy, in Patrick White's play, that it is not the passion of love that really matters, but loving-kindness. The hope is that loving-kindness will begin at home, and the garden will be a moat protecting it. Australians do not need to justify their preference for living in separate houses rather than in high-rise blocks. They do not want to be all over each other, literally or metaphorically. And there is also the fact that Australians are both quiet and reserved by choice, despite the democratic friendliness and the cheerful rowdiness. There is a profound respect for privacy.

In 1953 an acute French observer, Roger Loubère, whose book *Australie – Cinquième Continent* is almost unknown in Australia, noted that: *Another characteristic of Australians is that among themselves friends are always very discreet. This attitude is not one of indifference, but only of respect for your freedom; this custom makes social life all the more agreeable.*

This discretion and reticence, allied to the physical sameness of suburbia, helps to emphasize the impression of monotony among those who do not live in that particular suburb, or whose fate is to be different and yet to yearn for the reticence, the comforts of conformity. Roger Loubère stayed and worked in Australia long enough to see beyond the façade of monotony. His enjoyment of Australia was essential to his insight. He writes: *Although I was only a worker, my salary let me live well and my social condition did not prevent me from being invited into the best families. There exists all over Australia a democratic quality of life unknown in Europe, where social classes are separated by water-tight compartments, each ignoring the other, and where the luxury of a tiny minority exists side by side with the misery of the masses.* So his French-trained eye led him to look beyond sameness. *An American painter has called one of his works* Australia, *which shows the street of a suburb which never ends, and of which the houses all have the one veranda. It's true that there is an immense uniformity of manners and costume that is unknown in France, but this uniformity is like a canvas by a Van Gogh or a Monet. From the distance everything runs together; close up, each colour regains its rights, each line its character. After a certain time, one finds that the monotony is not as complete as it seemed . . . Basically the Australian is profoundly individualistic.*

Given the international pressures to standardize suburban Australians, in the products they buy, the TV programmes they watch, and the magazine articles they read, how is it that these people are so unmistakably Australian? (This includes millions of assimilated migrant families.) The answer is in the reality, not the myth, of the country itself, its sights and smells, and in the idiom of its inhabitants, the sound of Australian voices, the dead-pan jokes and comments on life, and in the gardens around the houses and in the beaches not far away.

That pernickety couple, Beatrice and Sidney Webb, made many acute and witty remarks about Australia in the 1890's, but they were so far from understanding its totality that their distance gives a sort of perspective. *Plain, mountain, undulating hill and dale, all alike covered with the monotonous Eucalyptus; glaring sun, everlasting winds carrying clouds of dust, dry nervous air, sickly colouring, the consciousness of the unreclaimable waste of the interior on the one hand, and of the interminable ocean on the other, gives to life in Australia a desolate combination of restlessness and ennui . . . On the other hand there is more enjoyment of life, a greater measure of high spirits among the young people of all classes. Australians are obviously and even blatantly a young race proud of their youth. Besides vulgarity and a rather gross materialism their worst characteristic is a lack of strenuous persistency: they are loosely built both in mind and body, incline to self-indulgence and disinclined for regular work.* Some of these comments are extraordinarily like those of D.H. Lawrence, 30 years later: *Always vaguely, meaninglessly on the go.*

The suburbs share with the countryside an appearance of monotony that disappears with knowledge, as *the monotonous Eucalyptus* is revealed to exist in more than 500 species. Their wild variety is known to the Supreme Court judge and to the lady who works in the hardware, as they plant *maculata* or *erythocorus* or *globulus*, and to the bank clerk and the engineer towing their caravans around the Flinders Ranges or the Atherton Tableland.

In 1952 the architect and critic Robin Boyd published a book called *Australia's Home* in which he wrote of suburbia as *a half-world between city and country in which most Australians live.* Boyd's eye was sharp but his judgement wrong. Suburbia is not a half-world but a world of its own, mistrustful of the city, deeply appreciative of the country and the sea, happy with its own idiom but no longer suspicious of the languages it does not know.

Brisbane suburban house on stilts.

House, Victorian country town.

Outback

'Outback' is a wonderful word, used in Australia for well over 100 years. The explorer Edward John Eyre wrote about 'The Back Country' in 1845. Australia is divided just so: Out, back; in, front. The cities are up there in front, in every way. Then comes the 'inside' country, the land of small paddocks and crops and sown pastures. Then comes 'the pastoral country', where the horizons are always further back. The paddocks get bigger, 100 acres, 1,000 acres, 20,000 acres, then they are reckoned in square miles, then measurements disappear altogether.

Not many Australians live outback, but most of Australia is outback. Henry Lawson, who didn't get very far into it, thought it hell. It certainly can be cruel, and is quite unforgiving of anyone who treats it carelessly. Yet its purity, its capacity to restore the soul, is quite extraordinary, like nowhere else on earth. It reminds me of the well in the medieval story, into which the sick eagle dives, to fly out again restored. Even the desert supports life, and little birds leave their code-marks on the sand, truths which can be read, devoid of deceit or thought of gain.

I was talking to a New Zealand doctor who had come to live in Australia. He told me he had visited Sydney and Melbourne for conferences, and didn't think much of them. They were just cities. Then some friends asked him to join them in a camping trip to Ayers Rock. He went, and was astounded. The whole journey was like nothing else he had ever known. So he brought his family to live in Australia, and whenever he can he takes them somewhere outback. His soul is refreshed, though being a medical man he says, *it clears out the system.*

When technology bangs in the Outback, it is noisy, incongruous and temporary. Then there is silence, and you can hear the birds. But you have to listen, for their sounds are as tiny as the cries of mice. One of the paradoxes of the Outback is that with all the vastness there is such a delicacy of detail, and you have to stop and be quiet to see and hear it.

For many years my family owned a sheep station, Uno, in the saltbush eight- to 10-inch rainfall country, 250 miles north-west of Adelaide; it was 453 square miles, which was not very big by Outback standards.

The homestead, set against the red rocky hills, was typical: a veranda on all four sides and a corridor straight down the middle. Out into the distance below the hills the soft greys and blues of saltbush, bluebush, mulga and myall stretched over the red earth. The manager, Jack Learmonth, his wife Pearl and their four children were all outback people. Jack and the boys could muster sheep through the mallee, the mulga and the weeping myall, and bring the mob exactly to the gate where anyone from 'the inside country' would be hopelessly lost.

Never go out of a fenced paddock when you're lost, was Jack's advice. Whereas it used to take weeks to muster on horses, now they did it in a few days on motor bikes. Boundary-riding was also made easier by motor bikes. The distances can be gauged by the fact that the bike did 75 miles to the gallon and had a one-and-a-half gallon tank and Jack always took a spare can.

Jack could do anything with those broad-thumbed bushman's hands that Russell Drysdale draws so unerringly. When I was a boy he showed me how to make silver initials on a whip handle, boring the holes so delicately and then pouring in the metal from a melted teapot, running smooth into the mould. Once he made a couple of bearings out of myall for the old Dodge tourer's engine, and she ran for thousands of miles on them.

Jack used to speak very fast, and take some liberties with language. Some of his words were not easy to interpret. *Galapigated* for *dilapidated* was simple, catching a *roo in a snooze* meant setting a snare to catch a young kangaroo. When my father once arrived at Uno, having had some trouble with the car on the way, Jack said, *Don't you worry, Mr. Dutton, it'll be either the carburetor wants adjustifying or the magneto wants regulizing.*

Parts of Uno were afflicted with that disgusting weed, horehound. Jack thought this an indelicate word to use in front of my mother, and always referred to it as *'og'ound*. This delicacy in front of women is very characteristic of bushmen. They could not be further from the Ocker cliché of the tough, swearing, insensitive boozer. Which is not to say they can't drink and swear when they want to. For some reason the word *bugger* is not regarded as swearing. *We're having a lot of trouble with the flies. Them buggers is bad this year.*

Jack had the bushman's sardonic attitude to those in authority. It was not his place to question them, but he knew what he knew, which was often more than what they knew, and more than he ever let on.

When the general manager, Mr. Lucas, came up from the South to superintend the siting of a new house on the station, the builder contended Lucas had got it wrong. *Don't worry*, Jack told the builder, *Mr. Lucas has a real good education and a real good compass, let him decide, old man.* The house was sited wrong.

People outback are at home with silence. After tea they will sit quite happily in opposite corners of the kitchen, just listening to the noise of the generator engine. They are also at home with patience. Jack would call up Pearl's cat, hold his hands out, and the cat would jump over them. *The sheep-expert taught him last shearing.* When it was time to turn the generator off, at 8 p.m., they would go to bed. But old Jack also loved to talk, and sing, and recite, and play the *button 'cordeen*, which is an accordion with buttons, slightly different from the *pianner 'cordeen*, which has keys. Jack and the three boys all played various instruments and they would go round the country playing at dances.

Like everyone in the country in Australia, their musical tastes were country-western. Their favourite singer was Chad Morgan, 'the Sheik of Scrubby Creek'. Unlike most country-western songs, his were triumphantly, full-blast Australian.

One year when we visited Uno, there was a woolshed dance at the end of shearing, for which Jack and the boys were playing. The floor was both rough in shape and beautifully smooth in surface from the wool; it was also a bit hazardous as it sloped down to the double doors where the yellow lamplight shone on the posts of the yards. One of the shearers had a wooden leg, but that didn't stop him from dancing; once he scooped up a 16-month-old baby from one of the women sitting by the wall and waltzed around with it. The mother did not stop him, but turned to my wife and said proudly, *It's a beautiful baby, and never cries.*

Jack loved to listen to the horseraces, and could recite ballads about horses for hours. He would stand straight up, lean slightly back, cross his right arm on his chest, and begin:

Rock gardener's dream, Flinders Ranges, South Australia.

A surfeit of cockles. The Coorong, South Australia.

Hold hard, Ned! Lift me down once more, and lay me in the shade.
Old man, you've had your work cut out to guide
Both horses, and to hold me in the saddle when I sway'd,
All through the hot, slow, sleepy, silent ride.

The singing and reciting sessions were usually in one of the boys' rooms at the back of the house. Pearl was never present, and perhaps this was a help, because some of Jack's favourite recitations were about burying Mother. He could moo like a cow on the first syllable of *Mo-ther*. In the first verse Mother died, in the second there was the coffin, the vicar, flowers and tears. The third verse was the grave. *Give Mum the flowers now.*

Jack had worked on the building of the East–West railway line. His stories about it were rattled out like an engine on full throttle. He always referred to the camps in terms of the number of miles from Port Augusta. *Once when the johns tried to poke their bib in on the two-up game, we just refused to take 'em on with us when we moved from the 370- to the 400-mile.* When he and his cohorts wanted to go to Port Augusta from the 500-mile for the races, they got the driver of the tea and sugar train tight on whisky, and they raced through all the stations without dropping the tea or sugar. Then they met the outgoing stores train at points. They argued who had the right of way. Finally their driver pushed the other train back across the points, and off they went to Port Augusta. *He was hauled over the coals for it too, the poor bugger, my word he was, old man.*

Another bushman who has been close to my family for many years is the primitive painter Henri Bastin. Henri, from Charleroi in Belgium, *where they talk the purest French*, jumped ship in Port Pirie in 1921 with two Greeks and an Englishman. Together they rode bicycles up the scalding track to Broken Hill where they found work. *Now*, says Henry, *those Greeks, they own cafe in Charleville; motel in Brisbane; two, maybe three cattle stations; garages. The Englishman, he owns biggest shop in Newcastle. Me, I own my bicycle!*

Henry had been an opal miner for years, as well as a shearer's cook, a mailman and a dozen other outback occupations. When he was working in Queensland for the eccentric millionaire station owner and art collector, Major Rubin, he began painting, using brand dyes and calico. The Major saw his work and was so impressed he bought him a set of paints and boards. Now Henri's paintings are each worth thousands of dollars and he has exhibited all over Australia and in the USA and UK.

One May we took Henri and his bicycle, tied on the station-wagon's roofrack, up towards the corner where New South Wales, Queensland and South Australia meet, to see his secret opal field. We set off for Mildura, with his bicycle on the roof, and a new pick and shovel, and his swag and blankets in the back. Henri's mixture of English, Australian, Aboriginal, French patois and his own abbreviations (e.g. *pape* for paper) takes some getting used to. As we got out into the mallee he talked faster and faster but more and more clearly about his adored back country, its flowers and trees and birds, and its opals and other precious stones.

Henri has a bad limp; he was shot in the ankle in World War I and taken prisoner. Amazingly enough the German doctor made him a silver plate for his ankle. As soon as we had stepped out on the red soil he headed off, right foot splayed out, saying his feet hurt on the city roads, and it was great to be out in the bush again. He looked on each tree as an individual, especially the weeping ones, the shea-oaks, the myalls and the wilgas, relishing their difference in shape, colour and texture. *Those artists in Melbourne, Sydney, Adelaide. They all paint the same tree.*

Back in the car, he talked more and more about opals and opal miners, he told about Canny Jimmy, who used to put all his pipe opals in champagne bottles and hide them; when Jimmy died, no one knew where they were. He told us about the first findings; about the South Africans who ground the opals up in their dollies, about the kangaroo shooter who was following a blood train and found a red stone; about the old-timers who used to bury their opals in mock graves, complete with crosses. *Out on your own you get very short of water. Best find water, you rub washing blue on your dog's paws and feed him lots of salt beef. Then when your dog finds water, you can track it back.*

We camped by a deserted bend of the Lachlan river, green-brown slow water way below the deep banks, white cockatoos screeching, green couch grass underfoot. Immediately Henri

limped off looking for grubs under the bark to use for bait for fishing. He was always close to the secrets of the country. In the morning before breakfast, he was off through the big fallen gums and came back saying, *Lots of mushrooms. What for we pick them we have good breakfast.* Off we went and filled the wash basin and a big curved piece of bark Henri had ready for them.

We drove on towards Bourke, the empty grey muddy road getting worse and worse. In the Outback you come upon road signs that must have been put up by some humorist, though they are fine, serious signs. At the turnoff to Houston, in the middle of nowhere, with one house and a shed across the road, there was a big sign *Beware of Pedestrians.* Before and after Gilgunnia there were two handsome signs announcing the town, but there was no town at all, only a few ruins and an abandoned mine on a hill. Driving down those huge, empty roads five or 10 chains wide for droving stock, a truck came straight at us, down the wrong side of the road. I was reminded of taking my test for my driving licence when I was 16; in those days in South Australia you got your licence first, then learned to drive. You had to answer half a dozen questions, none of which was: *Can you drive a car?* One of the questions was: *If you were driving down a deserted country road, which side of the road would you drive on?* I wrote down my honest answer: *Whichever side had the best dirt track.* The old Sergeant came over and glanced down at my answers. He put his finger on that one and said, *D'you come from the country, sonny? Yes,* I answered. *Well, cross that out and write 'Left'.*

On our trip towards Bourke, Henri had a story for every town we might ever come to. We must see the broken tree in Toowoomba, where the milkman killed himself, we must see the store in Cobar where the man blew himself up with his refrigerator. We must camp this night by the Warrego river, and catch lots of fish and crayfish. But we couldn't find the Warrego, and we couldn't risk driving too far over the sticky grey mud, which all along these western rivers of New South Wales comes thumping up from the wheels, and when you walk each shoe lifts up a lump the size of a dinner plate.

We camped by a billabong where I shot rabbits while Henri

Aboriginal rock carvings, Chambers Gorge, South Australia.

Goanna, desert, Western Australia.

went off to catch yabbies, those freshwater crayfish which in Europe are a delicacy and which in Australia can be caught by the bucketful. When it came to bedtime he got out his beautiful new hoe, scraped back all the coals of the fire, piled ash and earth where they had been, and spread green boughs, and over them stretched out his groundsheet and blankets. *Sleep warm this way*, ma foi!

It was a beautiful starry night with a tremendous dew. Henri was up very early looking for the Warrego. In the Outback nothing is so beautiful as the song of the birds at dawn, the native doves, the little grey woodpeckers, the choughs and currawong, but most of all the butcher birds, with their lingering call.

We drove north towards Cunnamulla through dreary swamps and along bone-shatteringly bad roads. Suddenly we were at the elusive Warrego, a beautiful slow stream beyond the reach of clean sand hidden below paperbarks with delicate frondy leaves, thick tufty moss and white gums across the river. Henri made a duck trap, and set off with buckets and lines for yellowbelly, the delicious fish of the northern rivers.

We stopped the night by a billabong, and Henri showed us the difference between the blue coolibah and the green cabbage gum with its wavy close grain, *Good for gunstock*. He threw a bough in the stream to catch shrimps, and picked up another piece of wood, his eyes lighting up. *Ah, Gidgee*, beautiful *wood for burning*. He talked about his times in Western Queensland, *Yes, plenty camel up there. Bad for fences*. He leaned back against a tree trunk and swayed from side to side. *Break down plenty fence post. Use plenty camel up there still*.

He stopped and pointed up at a little grey bird. *That very good bird, dogbird, always stay by baby, you never lose baby in bush with dogbird around; baby wander away in bush, dogbird stay by him*.

In the morning we were awakened by rain and had quickly to get the car out of our idyllic spot and on to the road. We went back for a swim in the river off the sandbank, the rain drops dimpling the water. When the rain starts in the back of Queensland that is the end of exploring. Henri's opal field was way out west of Charleville, past Quilpie and Eromanga, and with the rain coming down there was no hope of getting there. We slid onwards, over the mud of the main road, more sideways than forwards.

To cheer us up Henri said, *We get good feed at Charleville, my Greek friends own the cafe there*. But when we got there we found they had just sold out, to buy another motel in Brisbane. But the new proprietor knew all about Henri; we were given huge plates of steak and eggs, lettuce and tomato and beetroot, and were not allowed to pay for them.

Sadly we drove east towards Roma and Toowoomba and civilization. The bike would not be needed after all. Henri talked of the time he lost his bike for two days in thick mulga country. He found it by *spider web search*, which involves lighting a fire, then walking out for half a mile, turning right, walking 50 yards, turning right and walking back to the fire. He had gone almost right around the clock when he found the bike. Mais, *when you look for opal, you always light fire first, then you find your camp again.*

We stayed the night in a motel in Roma. In the morning Henri complained, Mais, *I had bad sleep. I am used to sleep on hard ground! When I roll over in these beds, I think I am falling into the creek. No ground under my shoulder.*

We left Henri at Toowoomba, where he had a daughter. When the weather improved he would take his bicycle and his new tools out 'home', 40 square miles west of Enomanga. He lifted his huge hand. *Nous avons fait un très bon voyage. Merci!* So we parted, in the pure French of Charleroi.

The famous loneliness of the Outback is, of course, genuine. People are fearfully isolated from each other, even with radio, aeroplanes and cars. But there are compensations, and probably most of those who live in the Outback are far less lonely than those who live in suburbia. Bushmen like Henri are never lonely because everything about them – rock, tree, bird, wind, water – means something to them. (Of course, Henri has the added advantage of being an artist.)

Meetings in the Outback last longer and go deeper than encounters in the city; strangers are relished and discussed long after they have gone. And there are the great occasions; the picnic race meetings, when people come in for days at an end from hundreds of miles away. We were once at William Creek, in the far

north of South Australia, shortly after the Gymkhana, for which 300 visitors had come from all over the Centre. There were races, dressage and auctions of horses. The owners of the lone hotel in William Creek had laid in 700 dozen bottles of beer, and the visitors brought their own as well.

William Creek is not far from Lake Eyre, out in the endless plain after the enormous bastion of the Flinders Ranges. In the distance Mount Termination looks like a ship at sea. In the treeless expanse bare stretches of gibber-coloured ground alternate with saltbush. The gibber areas look hard, but when you tread on them the crust gives way and underneath is bulldust, so fine that it penetrates the most tightly sealed cars. Lake Eyre itself is rather like a great piece of gabardine thrown over the earth, glinting light-stripes of salt, mustardy mud, the surface a crackly crust as hard as toffee.

It is a country of ruins, ruins of the old Overland Telegraph stations, some of which, like Strangways, look like medieval castles; the ruins of copper mines in the hills where once 1,000 men were working; ruins of an abandoned station. Even the hills seem ruined, like the Arkaringa Range where you walk over striated caps of rock perched on the top of crumbling hills of earth, and great sheets of gypsum-crystal that gleam like the wreck of 1,000 plate-glass windows. The vegetation, although constantly being renewed, suffers from droughts and over-stocking and shows endless ruins: black claws of dead saltbush, antlers and lizard-shapes of dead mulga. Then there are the ruined vehicles – such as the broken-down truck laden with Aborigines, like flies on a chop, dirt and smiles and laughter, the pale straw-coloured hair of the children blowing, the old men with red headbands asking for a cigarette. Aborigines never seem upset when their truck breaks down. They are neither in awe of machines nor obsessed with time as we are.

Some of the strangest ruins are those of the German Lutheran Missions at Kilalpininna and Kopperamanna on Cooper's Creek. German missionaries went up there in the mid-19th century, and learned the Dieri language, but later they abandoned the missions and trekked up to the Finke, where they established

Dead mulga, Northern Territory.

Frog in drought, Western Australia.

Hermannsburg. After the red rocks of the shaly, clattering Flinders Ranges, at Kilalpininna there is the smooth silence of the gold and white sandhills.

The mud and stone walls of the Mission buildings are crumbling and the sand is half way up to the doorframes, reaching to the twisted roof timbers cut from nearby trees. There is the endless debris of all abandoned outback settlements, flakes of rusted iron stoves and pumps and hinges, fragments of china and glass, the milky mauve or deep green of a thousand bottles.

In the Centre there are marvels as well as ruins. Ayers Rock and Mount Olga are as unforgettable as the Victoria Falls or the Grand Canyon. A couple of hundred miles south of Ayers Rock are the Everard Ranges, a whole valley full of giant red rocks, some of them scooped into deep pools at different levels in the rock, all full of water. In the dawn the dusty rocks turn to a fiery red, and parrots with blue bonnets and green chests fly past to the pools. Go west a couple of hundred miles and you are in the desert. Go east and you are past Oodnadatta and coming through shimmery black mirage-lakes of gibbers and the taut-skinned corpses of dead stock. The little gibbers fur the plains like iron filings over a magnet, and the big gibbers shine, polished by centuries of sand and wind. Beyond are the sandhills, the colour, said my daughter, of ground paprika.

A station homestead is like a little fort in its iron enclosure. Somewhere or another trees have been persuaded to grow about the house, ringed with earth and kept alive with washing-water. A cheery old lady is just back from town (Adelaide, 700 miles away). She can't stand the summers anymore, it's been 10 years without a summer rain, 187 points in the last 18 months, and a couple of Christmases ago it went up to 124° in the shade. (Dad stays on, he has been on the 'metho' for years, but he's alright now.) The blacks' camp is a few hundred yards away, a low triangle of galvanized iron with the entrances about four feet high.

On across the red sandhills and total desolation broken only by a few mulgas along the dry creeks, the red and black gives way to grey, white and yellow; there are treacherous troughs of hidden bulldust and you come upon the abandoned Dalhousie station, looking like a tiny Crusader castle in its solidity and loneliness.

The landscape looks more African or Middle East than Australian. Then suddenly there are the date palms (adding to the illusion) and the paper-bark teatree of Dalhousie Springs, an incredible nine square miles of oasis in the Simpson Desert. The water is the temperature of a lukewarm bath, and at dawn steam rises from it in clouds. There are thousands of ducks, majestic spoonbills flying off with their two black legs streaming behind, water birds, land birds of many kinds, and on the banks the thick-scented wattle is full of blue wrens.

Someone attempting to plumb one of the lakes ran out of line at 780 feet. Astonishingly enough there are little fish in Dalhousie Springs. I didn't realize this until I was sitting naked in the water having a shave in the morning and I was startled to have my manhood nibbled by half a dozen little fish the size of sardines.

Out beyond the springs there is the final desolation of the Simpson Desert, grey, white, saffron, square-topped hills, clay pans and sand. Yet there is life everywhere: dingo tracks for miles along the tyre marks of the oil exploration vehicles, brumbies standing back and watching, the stallion pacing around his mares with his long tail flying, lizards and even the accursed rabbit. Then the red parallel sandhills begin.

If possible, the Simpson Desert sandhills should be seen from a jet aircraft as well as from the ground. From 30,000 feet the detail becomes as fine as the shell of a walnut. Flying north-west you first see the watercourses radiating from Cooper's Creek, and the salt pans and dark vegetation are like stains on bark. The whole landscape seems to tilt down in the direction of the myriad creeks. Then the parallel sandhills begin; the peaks of the ridges, for 200 miles into the distance, glow deep red and the troughs are shaded a darker red, as if light were shining from underneath up to the rippling peaks. Then as you come out into firmer country the earth is paler between the still glowing ridges, straight now where earlier it had been combed.

Even in the Simpson Desert the sandhills carry quite a lot of vegetation. There are few totally bare areas in the Australian deserts. The cruellest is probably Sturt's Stony Desert, a flat and glittering expanse of gibbers. Drifting red parallel sandhills that usually seem devoid of all life recklessly burst forth in flowers and little trees after heavy rain.

We once drove from Alice Springs to Ayers Rock after a record season of rain. Eight years before, it had been bare as an ocean beach. Now there were miles and miles of yellow, white and pink daisies, magenta parakeelya that closes its petals in the late afternoon, golden cassia, the red and black of Sturt's desert pea, the purple of Sturt's desert rose, fat bobbles of mulga wattle, and young mulga coming up everywhere. Along the road there were the delicate pyramids of the desert poplar, a tree that grows as fast as if an Indian magician were breathing spells on it, its pink branches often topheavy with seeds like gum nuts. Beyond this the desert oaks hang down, and the mulga and cassia wirily poke up.

Perhaps the most beautiful of all areas in the Outback after rain is the vast network of channels and rivers leading down from Queensland to Lake Eyre. We drove up to the North Arm of Cooper's Creek in such a season. It was dry enough to move around again, which meant there had been time for the grass and clover to grow, and for the wildlife to come in and enjoy it all. After you lose sight of the sharp blue of the Gammon Ranges and Eyre's self-explanatory Mount Hopeless, you come across the stony plains to the shock of the Strzlecki creek, full of great stretches of water, its banks so like a beach that poor Sturt would really have thought he had discovered the inland sea he longed to find. In the morning a salt-pale dingo trotted along the other side of the creek and pelicans and swans were thick on the water. All the way from there to Innamincka there were mauve lawns of tiny flowers, and the deeper purple of a wild pea, and then you came to the magnificent pools of the Cooper, dense with ducks above and fish below, where Burke and Wills contrived to perish amongst healthy Aborigines.

Up the North Arm of the Cooper are the Coongee Lakes, miles of milky water, quite warm to swim in, to which a couple of boats had been hauled. The characteristic, indefatigable Australian will set off in an old Holden, towing a caravan or a boat, into some of the remotest regions in the world. It is extraordinary how seldom

Emu skeleton, central Australia.

Aboriginal burial ground exposed by the wind, the Coorong, South Australia.

he will come to grief, but if you have a four-wheel-drive vehicle you are often in demand to tow him out of sandy or muddy patches.

The caravan is the tangible proof of how much Australians have come to love their own country. Thousands of men retire at 60, or even 55, so they can set off with their wives for years of caravanning around Australia. One of the great functions of the Outback is this welcoming and healing of tired old city dwellers. Caravanners usually enjoy each other's company, but the great advantage of the Outback's size is that if you want to be on your own you can.

Up here by the Coongee Lakes, 800 miles from Adelaide, 1,000 from Sydney, there were dozens of cars full of children on their spring holidays. But where we camped by a billabong, the Cooper close by, we never saw a soul. The clover was ankle deep, the trees full of corellas, the water full of delicious yellow-belly. We had no bait, so I shot one of the hundreds of scavenging hawks, which floated down, wings extended. Its intestines made excellent bait. My wife and children counted 40 different sorts of birds near the camp, and always you could hear the tiny little noises of the scarlet finches, like a squeaking doll's house door. Nearby on the Cooper there were pelicans, ducks, swans, waterhens, egrets, spoonbills. St. Andrews Cross spiders hung enormous webs strong as nylon fishing lines across the trees. When we finally drove away two brolgas were dancing, then they ran forward and took off. A dingo bitch stood 20 feet away and wagged her tail at us. One set of dingo tracks went for four miles down the soft sand of the road.

The weather came up with thunder and broke, so we ran for Tibooburra. At the old Family Hotel there is an old friend of Russell Drysdale, who did some murals for him. Other artists followed, and out in this battered remote town, in the hotel, there are paintings by Clifton Pugh, Frank Hodgkinson and others, and a lovely painting Fred Williams exchanged for an Aboriginal artifact, since Fred was lame and unable to walk and look for it.

The thunderstorm had gone in the morning but there was no petrol to be had in Tibooburra. The proprietor of the Family amiably got out a drum and siphoned a tankful for us. *How many gallons d'you reckon that'd be?* he asked, trusting me not to cheat him.

We drove on and camped at Depot Glen, on Preservation Creek, where in 1845 Sturt and his exploring party were trapped for six appalling months and his second-in-command, James Poole, died of scurvy. We camped not far from his grave, and swam in the creek. Half a mile down the creek there was a big curved tree with steps cut in it, and strange initials and marks, surely made by Sturt's party. There in this ancient landscape human history is so close you can put your hand in its cuts, as on the Cooper Burke's message *Dig!* is still to be seen on the living tree.

Heavy rain at last enabled Sturt to leave Depot Glen. Often in the Outback it keeps people immobile. We talked to the son of a local station owner, who in hard times had taken to driving a mail and stores truck. In the country we had just come across, between the Cooper and Tibooburra, he was once caught in his two-wheel-drive Leyland by floods, and was stuck there for 11 weeks. *How did you survive?* asked one of the children. *Oh I was all right, I had a transceiver, plenty of stores, no worries. And no shortage of water!* Finally he was able to walk out of the flooded area, though the water was up to his chest for four miles. *Just as well I knew the track.* The truck he had left behind stood there for four months before he finally got it out.

The Outback is one of the driest regions on earth, and yet, unlike a sandy desert such as the Sahara, it has an intimate relationship with water. The rain, when it comes, greens it and flowers it. Below most of it lie the prodigious artesian basins from which the water roars up boiling. As the Aborigines knew, and explorers found out, birds are the messengers of water. One of the most delectable sights in the Outback is to come upon a station bore with a tank and great long troughs, and to see 4,000 or 5,000 scarlet and zebra finches, some of them sitting along the troughs rocking up and down to moisten their beaks in the water, while the rest wait along the rails of the yards. The air is full of a faint soft clicking as from a thousand distant knitting needles. They take no notice of you, waiting their turn for the water.

The Outback, however dry, magically gives such sustenance to human beings who come to sip from its richness. But it is as well to remember the finality of its terms. You find water or you die; human creatures are not like certain Outback lizards that never need to drink. There is a hawk hovering near the finches, and death is always present. Perhaps that is also good for the souls of city people, whose water is at the turn of a tap and whose food is waiting at the supermarket, and for whom death is the best-kept secret. The Outback has an enduring mystery and it keeps many secrets, but death is not one of them. Its message is spelled out in bones, white on the red sand.

Queensland crocodile.

Kingfisher, north Queensland.

The North

Few people, even Australians, think of Australia as being a tropical country. Yet an enormous area, which Xavier Herbert called Capricornia, lies north of the Tropic of Capricorn, encompassing much of Queensland, the Northern Territory and Western Australia. The line extends from the western Australian coast, about halfway between Carnarvon and North West Cape, through the iron mountain of Newman, across the Gibson desert, named in 1874 after the explorer Ernest Giles' lost companion, Alfred Gibson.

Giles, the most genial, the most poetic and perhaps the toughest of Australian explorers, who crossed the *prize and unrelieved* deserts of the west twice, left some of the most haunting descriptions of those regions. On his last journey, he was almost blind with ophthalmia and tormented by flies, his camels were sick and Giles finally admitted his fear. *The region is so desolate that it is horrifying even to describe. The eye of God looking down on the solitary caravan, as with its slow, and snakelike motion, it presents the only living object around, must have contemplated its appearance on such a scene in pitying admiration, as it forced its way continually on; onwards without pausing, over this vast sandy region, avoiding death only by motion and distance, until some oasis can be found. Slow as eternity it seems to move, but certain we trust as death; and truly the wanderer in its wilds may snatch a fearful joy at having once beheld the scenes, that human eyes ought never again to see . . . the nights I pass in these fearful regions are more dreadful than the days, for night is the time for care, brooding o'er days misspent, when the pale spectre of despair comes to our lonely tent; and often when I lay me down I fall into a dim and death-like trance, wakeful, yet 'dreaming dreams no mortal had ever dared to dream before'.*

His description cannot be bettered, because, despite his human audacity, he is open to eternity. White Australians, unlike the Aborigines, are not a religious people, but those who live in the Centre and the North especially are very much aware of death, and that itself is a kind of religion.

The Tropic of Capricorn comes across the Centre just north of Alice Springs and runs into Queensland across the Dingo Fence (the longest fence in the world, 6,000 miles long, enclosing a third of all Australia). It cuts through the town of Longreach and crosses the coast just north of Rockhampton, continuing over Heron Island. What a dry tropic it is! One might expect the Gibson and Canning deserts to be dry, but Longreach, in the heart of thriving pastoral country, has had droughts of 11 months in duration for one in five years since the 1890's.

Most of 'tropical Australia' does not look like the cliché picture of the tropics at all; there are no steaming jungles but plenty of pythons and crocodiles, hardly any paddy fields but plenty of water to grow rice or anything else. Much of what it grows is not for the benefit of man, but for the delectation of innumerable insects and thousands of birds. Most of Australia's North, outside the wet season, looks, and is, dry and hot, with a fierce light beating off the trunks of endless trees. Then all goes black for 50 miles, where the ground has been burned off by the Aborigines or station owners.

There are numbers of magnificent rivers – the Fitzroy, the Ord, the Victoria, the Roper – but no one has yet succeeded in making either them or the North useful for growing the white man's crops. The Ord river scheme, and lesser undertakings in the Northern Territory, have proved that anything can be grown; but the problem remains how the produce, or what is left of it after destruction by insects and birds, can be got to markets at a competitive price.

The more settled areas of the Queensland coast, from Rockhampton to Cairns and Port Douglas, are more conventionally 'tropical'. The palms along the white beaches, the pineapple and sugar farms, the pawpaws and mangoes make you feel you are in the tropics as you do not when you are on an 80-mile beach in Western Australia, say, between Port Hedland and Broome, with the Great Sandy Desert behind you.

When I was at boarding school in Victoria, there was a boy who came from Ingham, between Townsville and Cairns. He had a murderous great knife, used for cutting sugar cane, which he brandished when the boys called him Dago. This was an uncharitable reference to the numbers of Italians on the canefields, although he was plain (very plain) Anglo-Saxon.

For a long time Australians did not believe that white men could work in the tropics. 'Kanakas', as natives from various Pacific Islands were called, were brought in as indentured labourers, often abducted, or 'blackbirded'. Finally, there were so many outrages that the Kanakas were all sent home. Then the Italians, who were swarthier than the pink Anglo-Saxons, came in and worked the sugar. But of course it was all nonsense; any sort of white man can work in the tropics, even an Irishman, as long as he wears a hat. Australia was the first country in the world to prove this was possible. In other countries there were Negroes or coolies or Indians or Chinese to do the manual work, but in Australia, where the Aborigines were not interested in labouring, and the Kanakas were not allowed to, the white man had to do it himself.

Australians, especially Queenslanders, are so often attacked for being racists, that neither we nor anyone else has given us enough credit for getting out and working in the tropics. The real racist was the old European planter in the East or in Africa, sitting back in his bungalow sipping gin and tonic while the coloured labourers cut the sugar cane or the copra; or the modern executive, white, yellow or black, jetting in for a quick air-conditioned look at sweaty workers. The Australian may curse, calling them bloody Boongs, or worse, but he works and drinks alongside black or brown.

Clothes have been part of the battle. The old-style white man in the tropics had his panama and his white suit and his cummerbund; instead of accepting the sun, his pale skin steamed. Now it is hard to tell an Australian from a Polynesian or an Aborigine, working in a cane field or a pineapple plantation in nothing but shorts, brown skin and bare legs gleaming. From Broome to Cairns, everything else seems to come off with the clothes in a skin-to-skin directness of approach.

Australian audiences first had the shock of recognition of listening to their own idiom when they attended Sumner Locke-Elliott's *Rusty Bugles* and Ray Lawler's *Summer of the Seventeenth Doll*, both of which took their inspiration from the North. The cane cutters from *The Doll* have a fierce pride in their work *in the fields, near naked, black as pitch . . . sloggin' it out under the sun!* Their bodies are their tragedy; their splendid physical pride gone with age, the

Glasshouse Mountains, Queensland.

Snowy Mountains, New South Wales.

magic of the men whom their girlfriends had thought of as eagles is gone too.

Today, the coast of North Queensland has become the place to retire to. Age makes you welcome, because you come with your life savings. There are men still working in their shorts, of course, but there are also thousands of grandfathers and grandmothers, also in their shorts, far from their southern families, stretched out in deck chairs looking at the sun on the water. It is Senior Citizens' country, and its profile can be seen at evening when half a dozen old gentlemen are standing along the beach fishing, rods sticking out from the promontories of their bellies like a parody of lost youth.

But don't be fooled by the coast. Drive inland beyond the coastal mountains and there is harsh, dry and crackling Australia, offering no easy comforts to old or young. Nowadays you have to hunt for rain forests in the clefts of the mountains, for they have been sorely decimated by timber cutters seeking their beautiful hardwoods. The rain forests are the only luxuriant Australia, with whips of vine curling 50 feet or so over the ground and then shooting up to the tree ferns or orchids or strange birds' nests like a house of shingles.

Fortunately some of the rain forests that survive have jealous guardians. Once we drove an Australian and an American friend who had never seen a rain forest up into the mountains above Cairns that lead to the Atherton Tableland. Seeing a track going into the forest, I stopped the car and we climbed a dilapidated fence and walked down the green tunnel of the path, under booming pigeons and the crack of whip birds, our footfalls soft as the fallen leaves. It was so still and withdrawn one expected to see a giant python guarding its secrets. We turned back towards the road, and suddenly there was a little old man in shorts, with an enormous club, waiting for us in the middle of the path. We were trespassers, invaders, and would have been robbers if it had not been for the evidence of our empty hands. We apologized, but his fury lashed us like vines. Abruptly he said to me, *How far did you go down the track?*

Only to the bottom of the first hill.

He glared at me. *You missed the best bit. There's a creek at the bottom. Usually a python there.*

He had completely changed now he was the guardian of the treasure, lovingly displaying it for all of us. He told us that this couple of hundred acres of rain forest belonged to him, but that he had to fight to protect it from developers and timber cutters who wanted to flatten it, and vandals and thieves who wanted to rob it. Sometimes they would come armed with 30-foot secateurs to snip the orchids off the trees.

Look, he said softly. We turned round. A cassowary and her chick were coming down the path towards us. She stopped close by us and watched, darting the enamelled splendour of her head. Then the chick dashed off into the forest and she followed.

Long may that old man continue to guard his rain forest. There are too few like him in Queensland.

For the visitor, North Queensland is very confusing, because everything seems to happen at once, like chrysanthemums and phlox flowering together. On one side you see men planting young shoots of cane and on the other they are letting fire rip through walls of standing cane, so that all the dry stuff is burnt, leaving only the dry tops and the tuft, high on its shanks, striped black and white like convicts.

Like all crops, cane is ruthless to the landscape. You have to head for the hills to recover wild Queensland, or go to a creek running through the padded softness of paperbarks. There, invisible crimson lorikeets are chirring in the highest branches, drongoes and peewits are more obvious, and occasionally you see a flashing wren.

The lack of any sense of time extends to the towns from the country. There are hardly any old buildings, but since most of them are wood age would be a contradiction; all the cities north of Rockhampton give the impression that they were begun in the 1930's and are still being built. You look at the people in the streets in their minimal clothes, so fresh and friendly, and wonder whether they too have any past.

Port Douglas, north of Cairns, is an exception. It has a 19th-century style and elegance, and the past is proclaimed by the effrontery of a statue and marble column with a water faucet, in the middle of the main street, honouring a German pioneer. If you read the inscription you find out that Mr. F.D.A. Carstens (1838–1906) was *A vigorous advocate of the construction of the Mossman Tramway. Chairman of the Port Douglas Hospital Committee 1892–3.*

The real proof of the past, of course, is in the cemeteries. Remote Australian cemeteries are endlessly touching, with their markers for children who died, so many and so soon; the wives at childbirth or from later fevers; the men young and old, murdered by blacks, killed in mine explosions, or dead from the weather and the wrong clothes and no medicine. They tell the common story of white men, women and children in the 19th century, trying to adapt to living in the North of Australia, and paying an appallingly high price. Those 90-year-old gravestones at Port Douglas, from that little settlement more than 1,000 sea miles from Brisbane, could be transferred across the continent to the ghost town of Cossack, more than 1,000 sea miles from Perth, though more sand blows at Cossack, the rocks are harsher and there is no rain forest near or far.

At Port Douglas there is one tombstone for three dead, Thomas Ellam's beloved wife Mary Teresa who died 4 February 1888, aged 22 years, and their children Charlotte Teresa, who died 12 February 1888, aged two years six months, and Thomas who died the year before, 14 days old. At Cossack it was a wife who lost her husband and her children, including *My Dear Little Alex, who died April 7th, 1886, aged nine years and seven months.*

Other stones are more mysterious, like one at Port Douglas for William Thomson who *met his Death by Cruel and Treacherous Murder on the 22nd day of October, 1886.* But it is the children and the young mothers and fathers who are the most poignant.

*　　　*　　　*

For most of its length you would never know that the North Queensland coast is guarded by the greatest reef in the world, for it is so far out to sea. It was first navigated, with consummate skill, by Captain Cook in 1770.

'Now the shearing is all over . . .' Gong, outback shearers' kitchen.

The stockman's last bed.

Australians have a passion for these islands and atolls, and the tourists swarm to them from Lizard Island beyond Cooktown, down to Green and Dunk and Hayman and Heron and Fraser, which are all shapes and sizes, but basically offer the same sun and sea and reefs. Apart from their obvious beauty, these islands are tiny refuges from the enormous scale of Australia. Instead of feeling trapped, people seem to feel secure. There is also a special sort of camaraderie, like being on a ship. A friend who once worked as a waitress on Heron Island said that almost all the guests (not to mention the staff) suffered severely from what was known as 'Heronitis': the uncontrollable urge to spend the night in someone else's bed.

The islands also offer a flattering mirror of sophistication. We first visited Hayman Island only a year or two after its hotel was opened, back in the 1950's. With a group of friends we had chartered a launch and were cruising in the Whitsunday Islands, and to the Outer Barrier, catching all those glorious northern fish, red emperor, coral trout, spanish mackerel, kingfish. The whales were in procession down the coast, spouting and playing with their young; sometimes a mother would flick her baby high into the air to land with a smack and a splash you could hear and see a mile away. We landed on Bushy Atoll on the Barrier, where a sea eagle sat on a low tree watching us pick up shells. With mask and snorkel I dived into a cave in the reef and came face to face with a 500-pound groper, which the divers fear more than sharks. I shot out backwards as fast as I could. Looking at its huge mouth, I remembered Mrs. Beeton's recipe for cooking groper: *Do not omit the thick gelatinous lips, as these are a delicacy*.

We fished in greater luxury than I have before or since; at night we sat on deck, a glass of brandy and a cigar to hand, the line streaming out on the tide, the coral trout flashing rosily as we pulled them up out of the black water. One night we landed at Hayman Island and had dinner at the hotel. The determined efforts to be elegant and sophisticated jarred after the easy-going but genuine life on board our boat. After dinner I asked the barman for six brandies. He brought them in tumblers and barked *Sodaorginger. Neither*, I said. *We've just had our dinner and we want a brandy with our coffee.* He swept the tumblers up, glared at me for my crudity and said witheringly, *You shouda asked for* cognac.

This sophistication is now on an international scale on some of the islands. Film stars like Lee Marvin come for the marlin season, and the cognac is all VSOP. At Mission Beach, near Dunk Island, we were talking recently to a rangy, bearded local, his bare limbs like sandal straps, his back like Spanish leather. He had been piloting one of the big boats out around the Barrier for a group of fishermen from the south. *Bloody beautiful boat, Jeez, was it ever: 75 feet, twin diesels, 1,400 horse power, 59 gallons an hour, 30 knots. That's the life, and they pay for it, $1,000 a day all in for two weeks. And Jeez, watcha get, the skipper runs the boat for you and takes you to the fish, the deckies settle you in a chair, pull the tops off the stubbies for you, bait the hook, gaff the fish. The birds get into the spirit of it, get their tops off and dive off the tower. Then when you come back to the wharf they're waiting for you with champagne and prawn cutlets. Jeez, that's the way to do it, but you gotta be rich. On our boat we had two doctors, a dentist and a real estate man. That's where the money is!*

Fortunately you don't have to be rich to enjoy the North Queensland islands. We went for the day on a launch from Port Douglas to Low Island, with about 40 other people jammed onto the 40-foot boat, skippered by a round-faced, jolly Thursday Islander. The passengers were all middle-aged to old, battered and happy.

Our fellow passengers on the old launch were the salt of the earth: Lawson's *the men (and women) who made Australia.* The two ladies sitting on the coil of rope next to us talked of their husbands, and men in general, as 'they'. *They've worked so hard all their lives, much better to retire at 55 healthy than at 65 with a stroke or a heart attack.* One woman said she and her husband drove off every year from Sydney in their camper-van Ford. On their last trip to Cairns four years ago, they went back through Alice Springs for the wildflowers. *You'd see a dozen different varieties in a yard or two. Absolutely beautiful.* On the other side a jolly woman from Adelaide was talking about the nude bathers at Maslens Beach, some of whom had complained at being photographed. *I mean, if they want to take their clothes off, that's their business, good luck to them, but they shouldn't mind anyone else having a look at them. More of it the better, I think, it'd do away with all this sex and raping.*

The Thursday Island skipper brought us into the lagoon at Low Island, which consisted of a blinding ring of sand and emerald and peacock water, with a lighthouse, a couple of houses and some vegetation. We were deposited on an atoll, everybody with heavy shoes against the coral as well as buckets and sacks and assorted tools for extracting anchored shells. Our fellow passengers streamed off across the reef, with its utter desolation of old, dead coral; the greys and browns of living coral out of which flash all the vibrant colours of fish and shells; the viridian and purple mantle of clams; the sponges; the sand-marked seaslugs; and a brown striped creature like a snake, with a fronded mouth, that when I gingerly picked it up was hollow like a bicycle inner tube.

Five hours later we were all back on board again, comparing finds. We had three lovely huge spider shells, one for each of the children. No one had been spiked by a stone fish or slashed by a cone shell. The lady from Sydney had a big bailer shell which she was going to swap for some cones from a friend at home. Sooner or later, I suppose, this largesse will come to an end, and already shell hunting is not allowed on islands like Heron that have thousands of visitors a year. But Australia's beaches and reefs are so immense that anyone who gets away from the crowds can still find wonderful shells. And if you know someone on a prawn trawler, or a pearl lugger, then you can find the volutes and others that come up from the depths.

*   *   *

My sister Helen is an expert shell collector who has written a text book on shells of the Northern Territory. She is also a pilot, and she flew my wife and myself out across Arnhem Land, past the English Company's Islands, to the Wessel Islands which are as far north as you can get in Australia. If you come towards Arnhem Land from Darwin you cross the two Alligator rivers and other streams, and you see different colours of water

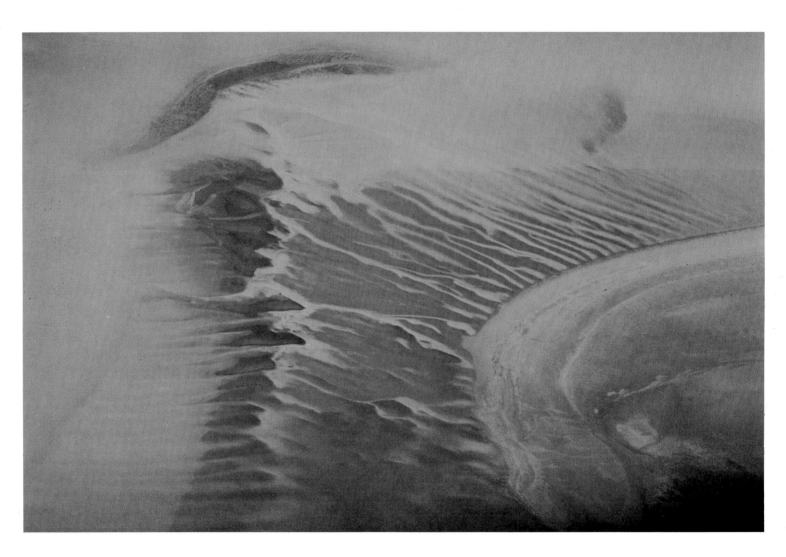

Sand sculpture, Broome, Western Australia.

Shell sculpture, giant clam, Great Barrier Reef.

together, the milk-coffee-fresh water meeting the green salt water. There are nameless black streams and deep chasms in the hills, blue pools by rock and sand, and the marbled blue-green-brown of the estuaries. There are huge flocks of white ibis and spoonbill, and buffalo everywhere in the green plains and black soil swamps, sometimes swimming or wading through lakes trailing a wavering V of mud-stained water behind. Then comes the tremendous escarpment, the stacked rocks infiltrated by the green of rivers and trees, sometimes squared off as by giant masons.

Down at Maningrida in the thick heat one of the Aboriginal artists, Jumbo, let us watch him paint, explaining what he was doing in a soft, gentle voice. He had a long, very humorous face and curly hair; he was stripped to the waist with a tremendous cicatrice across his chest. He was a woodcarver as well as a painter. Everything he did – the colours he used, the bark or wood he painted on, the legends he depicted – was of a piece with his own country. When tribal Aborigines talk of Land Rights, they are not talking of land as something you own, but as something that gives your spirit life.

We took off and flew over enormous anthills that look like ruined monuments, or like buffaloes and their shadows. We crossed splendid Blue Mud Bay, accurately called so by Matthew Flinders. (Indeed, Flinders' charts of this coast are still in use.)

Groote Eylandt with its manganese, and Nhulumbuy (Gove) with its bauxite, have mining towns that could not look more different – B.H.P.'s Groote Eylandt all spaced out wide under trees, Nhulumbuy quite European-looking, with white blocks of flats. The impact of the mines on Aboriginal life has likewise been quite different in each place, the tribal Elders at Groote Eylandt having done a much better deal with B.H.P. than the Yirrkala with the International Consortium at Gove.

Although the issue of uranium mining has divided the Aborigines as well as white Australians, the general mineral wealth of Arnhem Land has given the Aborigines there a base of power that others lack. Traditional Aboriginal society is not structured to cope with such power in terms of Western managerial direction. But Arnhem Land has already produced a remarkable political leader in young Gallarwuy Yunupingu.

Sometimes it is a relief to get away from both white and black. Great, healing Nature is waiting in Australia with arms open, as long as you are prepared to travel distances and not expect her to offer you food and drink.

Our Arnhem Land flight with my sister was to continue over the uninhabited islands of the English Company's (named by Flinders after the East India Company) and Wessel groups. These are extraordinarily beautiful and diverse, and quite different from the islands off the coast. Any one of the English Company's islands would make a perfect refuge. They have everything. A white beach on one side, cliffs, folded hills, trees, flowers, and on the other side a miniature river with smooth curves and mangrove-defined banks. The Wessels are another shape altogether. They are flatter, with a low scrub, and have an extraordinary table of rock that looks as if it had been incised by a giant Aborigine into the walls of a tjuringa stone. Some of the cuttings are only a few feet deep. Others go down to the water, leaving saw-toothed cliffs. Vicious tide-races run between the islands, curling and swinging in clear currents when seen from the air.

One island is cut right through by a narrow passage known as The Hole in the Wall. A friend of my sister, a Greek trader who supplies the settlements and islands in Arnhem Land, finally took courage and steered his schooner into The Hole in the Wall. The wheel was useless, the big diesel powerless, and the 85-foot boat swung right round, bow and stern just missing the cliffs, and went through backwards. It was an exploit worthy of that other Greek sailor, Odysseus, going home to Ithaca.

We landed on the last island of the Wessels on a short hump-backed strip by the unmanned weather station. It was grey as Tasmania, but very warm. The vegetation that looked drab from the air was in fact full of flowers – big pink ones, the shape of roses; yellow ones that seemed to grow from the tips of the leaves of an oak-like bush; a purple pea; and everywhere pink and white convolvulus.

We got up at 4.30 a.m. to catch the low tide and went out on the reef with torches. My sister nonchalantly warned us to keep an eye open for sharks, stingrays, octopus, stonefish and, of course, the deadly sting of the very cone shells we were looking for. The reef was alive with all these offerings, and more. My wife cried out with excitement, and I went over to her, and saw that she had found four painted lobsters, all sitting around a rock waving their whiskers at her. I grabbed one, which was striped all over with colours from rose pink to green to blue to yellow. Later it seemed an act of vandalism to boil him red, but not when we ate him, hot with melted butter.

We flew back to Darwin via the Cobourg Peninsula; with its bays and beaches and forests and undisturbed wildlife, it is one of the most beautiful places in all the North. The Ranger took us in his boat to the ruins of Victoria, which was the third abortive northern 'capital' before Darwin, in the harbour of Port Essington. Established in 1838 and abandoned in 1849, it was visited by John Gould, the natural history artist, by Ludwig Leichhardt on his 1844–5 expedition, and by T.H. Huxley on the *Rattlesnake* in 1848. It was Huxley who declared it to be *About the most useless, miserable, ill-managed hole in Her Majesty's Dominions.*

Unless you know where to look, you would not find Victoria now, amidst the gums with their big heart-shaped leaves. From the boat you see a high cream and red cliff, the only one for miles, standing out by a low point of mangroves that turns out to be the old causeway. Then up in the scrub, amongst the orange blossoms, there are the squared stones of the huge, round Cornish chimneys, still red though blackened by fires. There are also bits of best dinner services from the officer's table of the 1840's, huge bottle tops, and a powder magazine that is still perfect, containing nothing but a dead goanna, with a tree growing out of the roof. It is stiflingly hot, an airless place, and one thinks of the convicts in their heavy clothing who built it, the officials in their uniforms, their ladies swathed in muslin, and John Gilbert in 1840 bringing specimens back for Gould. (Five years later, Gilbert was murdered by Aborigines from the Mitchell river. At the time, Gilbert was guiding Leichhardt to Port Essington, and the Aborigines in their party molested the Mitchell river women.)

Road train outside Western Australian pub.

Landrover's burden: grasshoppers, Western Australia.

The North-West is perhaps the most fascinating part of the North, in terms of its scenery, its potential for producing food and energy, and its already thriving mines, especially of iron ore in the Pilbara. The new towns, such as Tom Price, Dampier, Karratha and Kunnunura, are extraordinary suburban oases, sprinklers putt-putting over lawns, the hotel dinner menu in both French and English. A few miles away and you are alone in an untouched landscape under an enormous, unpolluted sky.

We flew from Perth to Carnarvon by jet, and then drove, with some detours, to Darwin. The jet-height air yields the vastness of Western Australia, from Nullarbor to Albany, and north from Geraldton, in those pale tracks that slice the dark scrub and move on toward the farthest horizon, which from 30,000 feet *is* a far horizon. There is an almost frivolous gaiety in the blue and green and gold of the coast. Carnarvon itself tells another Western Australian secret, that of water hidden beneath the ground. Its huge irrigated plantations feed Perth (typical of our insane age, vegetables and fruit for Carnarvon go down to Perth and back again, a distance of about 1,200 miles, to feed Carnarvon). Yet the water comes from bores below a dry river, the Gascoyne, which in flood is a mile wide and up to the tops of the trees. The floods come from 500 miles inland, and there is normally a two-week warning; then everyone goes out to the 10-mile bridge for a barbecue and the first one to spot the wave coming gets a prize.

Ken Watters, an agent in Carnarvon, had been skipper of a prawn trawler. He talked of a record catch of 38,000 pounds, and of the day they filled 80 bags with scallops and could have done many more if the crew had not hidden the remaining bags. But the markets are soon glutted by scallops and snapper and mullet, and the boats lie idle. One of the most unsatisfactory things about Australia is the national failure to develop the fishing industry.

A few days later, on the beach at Dampier, we met a girl walking her dog. She was from Queensland, but *I'm really rapt in Dampier*. She was the perfect Australian girl, sexy if not quite beautiful, tough without being coarse, devoid of hangups, wonderfully wholesome. She had been out fishing the day before with her husband and had caught 80 pounds of Spanish mackerel, queenfish and coral trout, and on the way home she herself had caught a 40-pound Spanish mackerel. They were giving up their jobs and going down to operate a prawn trawler from Exmouth. *I'm really rapt in fishing, and besides, it's my duty to him, it's his big chance. Besides, it's a good life, if you can stand up to it, and you eat well.* Ken said the regular breakfast was four prawn cutlets, a hunk of fish, a few scallops, squid, chips, eggplant and zucchini. The sea is full of fish and prawns. *And all the rubbish*, says Ken, *sharks, stonefish, shells, seasnakes and assorted fish.*

The land itself – at Mount Tom Price, Paraburdoo, Mount Newman and Goldsworthy – is full of minerals, and there are ports for shipping the ore at Dampier, Wickham and Port Hedland. The story of the Pilbara is typical of Australia's extraordinary under-confidence in its own potential. In 1882 a geological inspector from the Western Australian government visited the Pilbara, as far as was possible in the days before aeroplanes, and reported: *It is essentially iron country. There is enough to supply the whole world.* Nothing was done about it, and in 1938 the Federal Government even banned the export of iron ore.

All through the steel-hungry 1950's the embargo continued, despite Lang Hancock's appeals after a flight from Hamersley to Perth during which bad weather had forced him to fly low between the cliffs of the Turner river in hitherto inaccessible country. What he saw convinced him that the cliffs were solid hematite.

The embargo was lifted in 1960, and within two years Hancock and his partner Peter Wright had persuaded Rio Tinto of Great Britain and Kaiser Steel of the United States to come and look at the Pilbara. Tom Price, a vice-president of Kaiser, flew over it and said: *I think this is one of the most massive ore bodies in the world. There are mountains of ore there.* He died the next year, but the mine called after him is now the biggest iron mine in the world. Most of the ore, processed into pellets at Dampier, goes to Japan, though Japan has now reduced its orders, and the pellet works will close.

Those who complain about multi-nationals must realize that Australia alone could never have afforded to build the Port of Dampier and the railway to Tom Price, nor could it have mined the iron or built the town for the workers. But it's no less disturbing that no one knows how much of Australian mining is owned by foreigners; the most reliable estimates run between 50 and 60 per cent. Lang Hancock wants Australia to build a railway from Queensland to bring coal for a steelworks near the Pilbara. He says it would cost only $350 million and would give work to thousands of unemployed. Maybe he is right. As it is, he and Wright each draw about $5 million a year in royalties from the Pilbara.

The 60-mile drive between Tom Price and Wittenoom offers the most ravaging contrasts I know between the old and the new capitalism. In Tom Price there are green ovals and public gardens and low dividing walls beautifully built from local stone which comes away from the hills in neat sections as if already cut. Bearded fathers in shorts ride up to the supermarket on bicycles with a child on the luggage carrier. The huge bar at the hotel is full of miners in shorts, and an old solitary playing pool. Outside, red dust-smothered Landcruisers stand alongside clean suburban cars. In the cool hush of the supermarket you can buy almost anything; even a pack of four bottles of Schweppes soda water, for $1.11. On the hotel menu there is smoked salmon and *foie gras* and the rosy-cheeked waitress has difficulty with the lengthy wine list. There is a large library, and an excellent hospital and school, though further schooling is a problem in all these remote towns.

Out at the mine is a second town, as there always is near these little Canberras in the bush. This is made up of hundreds of air-conditioned boxes, like little white coffins, that house the single construction workers. By way of compensation, their wages and benefits are prodigious, and they enjoy all the facilities of the town.

Driving to Wittenoom from Tom Price in early October is like taking a journey through Sidney Nolan's Paradise Gardens. All the flat, red, bare areas between the scrub are packed with flowers. The bigger eremophilae, often called Emu bush, or poverty bush because they can hang on through drought, are six feet high, and curving, bell-shaped flowers run all the way from blue to purple to yellow to deep pink. Bow-taut lizards scuttle between them. Over them an eagle is being harried by crows.

The geometry of roads . . .

. . . North-west Western Australia.

Then, out in the bare, hot plain, you come to Wittenoom Gorge, a dust-shrouded town of empty houses with bashed-in asbestos walls and broken windows. Other than the ghosts, only a few lonely looking people still live there. The road leads into the Gorge itself, one of the most beautiful in Australia, with its high red cliffs and deep pools of water, all polluted with junk, rubbish, broken machinery, rusty galvanized iron and thousands of broken sheets of asbestos.

Lang Hancock began to work the blue asbestos in the 1930's, then sold out to a subsidiary of Colonial Sugar Refinery. By 1960 the mines had closed, and the workers were dying of asbestos dust in the lungs. Now the Western Australian government wants to close down the town itself because of the danger from the asbestos fibre.

In the heart of the Gorge is a rest camp of pleasant houses and gardens, with a Range Rover and a Jaguar in the carport by the biggest house. It all belongs to Lang Hancock, who occasionally comes for a visit with friends. The only inhabitant is a rather disconnected old man, who is gardener-cum-caretaker. I asked him if there were any plans to clear up the ruins of the mine buildings and the rubbish in the Gorge. *Huh*, he replied.

A couple of hundred miles from this dreadful place, through ramparts of rocky ranges and spinifex plains, you come to the new world again. There is the port of Dampier and the administrative centre of Karratha, houses and gardens, speedboats in the carport, and oysters, prawns and lobster for dinner at the hotel. The chief problem here for ordinary people, and small businessmen, is to keep up with the mining company's benefits. At Dampier the workers, already on huge salaries, get a furnished house, free electricity and water, and free maintenance for about $9 a week. The single men in the construction camp get all their meals, and their room cleaned, for $36 a week. What private individual or small firm could compete?

And tucked away somewhere, especially at nearby Roebourne, are the Aborigines, who do nothing. Occasionally you hear of a bright success, an Aboriginal who enjoys working as a gardener for the mining company, or a team under the leadership of the naturalist Harry Butler's son Trevor, who shoot wild goats and sell the skins and the meat for pet food. But this is a rare story.

The suburban order and neatness is real enough, but it is a veneer. An old, established town like Port Hedland is nearer reality, rich and comfortable in parts, rough and old-style North in others, with Aborigines at all levels. In the great bar of one of the hotels a station owner is talking about the last cyclone. It blew down 23 windmills, demolished 100 miles of fencing, and washed away half his stock. *The horses just kept backing away from the wind and they ended up in the Indian Ocean.*

Violence is part of life in the North, on land, on sea, in the air, in the fists and jaws. And in war. Most Australians never knew of all the Japanese air attacks on Broome and Wyndham and other targets. With typical lack of confidence in the Australian people, our leaders thought we might panic if we knew. As it was, the army were excelling themselves, doing things like knocking out the Port Hedland blowholes in the rocks by the sea so the Japanese could not use them as landmarks. The Japanese, who had been pearling along this coast for years, had no need of landmarks, for they knew every inch of the coast.

In the years before the war, the old ship, the *Manunda*, that traded up the coast from Perth to Broome and Wyndham, once went out in a cyclone to rescue the crews of a Japanese pearling fleet. For this heroic act, the Emperor presented the ship with the Order of the Chrysanthemum. When the bombing began, time and again the Japanese planes came over and sank everything in sight but they never touched the *Manunda*.

Broome is one of the most rewarding towns in Australia, not only for its natural beauty and its history but for its thriving multi-racial community. *Broome cream*, an old resident murmured approvingly as a very pretty girl walked past; she was probably a mixture of British, Japanese and Aboriginal, with perhaps a dash of Chinese, Philippino or Malayan as well. Broome is classically tropical, with its houses of deep verandas and shuttered shades, its wide streets and flowering trees and gardens, and a milky sea beyond the mangroves.

On the way from Port Hedland to Broome we had stopped, like everyone else, at the petrol station at Sandfire, half way along the 400 miles of dusty road, for petrol and a cold beer. The proprietor, Eddie Norton, gravel-voiced, with a fine face and a large tobacco-stained moustache, beer belly hanging down over unbuttoned shorts, was a highways worker who had correctly deduced that 400 miles is too far for most cars to travel without refuelling. After resigning from his job, he and his wife went half way between Port Hedland and Broome, in the scrub of the Great Sandy Desert, and, as he says with bush irony, *We carried out a feasibility study*. By that he means that they lived in a spinifex shelter and sank a bore and found abundant water. Now they have their petrol station, restaurant and bar, motel rooms and a beautiful garden. There is another row of transportable rooms, *for drunks*, Eddie says. *You can't let the poor buggers out on the road after 10 p.m., so I shove 'em in there.* He then pointed to three little children by a caravan – *my brumbies* – whose mother, a Malayan girl married to an Australian, had been murdered a few days ago. Before returning to his bar, Eddie insisted on holding up the hose for us to feel and taste the bore water and admire its clarity.

The barmaid was a beautiful brown-skinned girl, severe yet cheerful. Sitting next to us was a truckie, Doug James. He was on his way to Darwin and bought us a drink. *What speed do you drive?* he asked my wife. *About 60–70. All right, I'll see you up the track.*

The next evening at Broome I had filled the car with petrol and was about to drive away when I realized how spattered with bugs the windscreen was. I stopped to clean it, and a minute later there was a sigh of air brakes as a huge Mercedes semi-trailer pulled up beside us. A voice from on high called down to us. It was Doug.

He introduced us to his mate Moose, who was brown as the dust, had a bare torso, bare feet and a battered pair of shorts, but was a serious man under the banter. Moose was an ex-trucker who now ran a vegetable farm on the outskirts of Broome. He wanted to show us some pieces from an old wreck he and a friend had discovered down the coast, by a rock with the date 1795 carved on it.

It was 5 p.m. and it seemed Moose and Doug were already due at the farm, but they took us out to the hut of the man who ran the

The art of camouflage: Western Australian spider . . .

. . . *Queensland leaf insect.*

caravan park and who also had some relics of wrecked ships. We sat and drank with him, his glass eye gleaming but his good eye wary. An unpleasant young man came to the door of the caravan wanting to buy some beer. He was told the shop was closed. Threats began to dribble out of his loose face, and Doug and Moose leant forward. *My mates will be pissed off with me*, he said. *Ladies present*, snapped Doug. *What's wrong with pissed? Anyway I could drink you under the table*, he boasted to Moose. *Yeah? A carton of stubbies straight? Yeah. But not with whisky chasers!* laughed Doug. The slob slunk off. Doug told us later that Moose used to do the 400-mile run out into the desert to a gold mine, on a dead-straight bulldozed track. *Only way he could get through was to take an iced carton of stubbies and a waterbag full of whisky.*

We finally got to Moose's farm at nine, to a very hostile reception from his brother and sister-in-law and friends who had been waiting since five. Later, after a barbecue of spare ribs and stingray, Moose showed us the pieces from the wreck. There was a massive mast ring (the experts from the Museum at Perth said the ship must have been about 800 tons), gaff lift and other rusted bits. The anchor, with the rest of the wreckage, was still wedged in the rocks.

We then inspected the farm with torches. Moose had bought six acres and a draught-horse, half Clydesdale and half Percheron, and did all the ploughing with two ancient single-furrow ploughs. His 'vegies' were superb. He and his wife and seven children lived in two caravans, and he had just bought a surplus hut from the aerodrome for a house. *I reckon the kids ought to know how this country was built*, he said when we found the old horse. His children obviously adored the whole farm, complete with donkeys, a pig and geese.

Moose was a philosopher, and not only about his farm. He patted the bull-bar (called kangaroo bars on cars) on Doug's truck. *Bit of a dent there on the corner*, Doug pointed out, *where I hit a buffalo last trip. Roos?* he laughed. *They go straight under. I used to run 'em all over*, said Moose. He was not the only one; there were hundreds of dead kangaroos along the road. *But one night I thought, 'animals have as much right to live as us.' After that I always blew the horn, that sets 'em*

thinking, then I turn out the lights for a second or two, that lets 'em clear off. Since doing that I never hit more than a couple, instead of hundreds.

Have a Kimberley cold, said Doug, handing me a stubbie of warm beer.

They yarned on about the time there was a row of hippies asleep in the truck bay and Doug just managed to pull up short of them. Another time the automatic steering went wrong on the giant Euclid earthmover, and it chased a poor bloke all over the embankment they were building. *Never seen a man run like it. He went up a 60-degree bank with me right after him, couldn't do a thing. Finally managed to jam the front into the ground. Took a morning to get it out again.*

Doug recalled the time Moose got annoyed with three new young coppers in Hedland who were picking on the kids and beating them up. *He finally jobbed all three of them*, said Doug with relish. *That's right*, said Moose. *I was released on $1,000 bail. Had to finish a job out to Woodie in the desert. I lost third gear on the old Leyland. Had to wire to the Flying Doctor that I couldn't show for the court case. I got back to Hedland a fortnight late, expecting jail. The old sergeant told me, one, he'd got the bail lowered to $16; two, the case had been dropped. Shortly after, two of those three coppers were booted out of the force.*

In the North distance is a bond as well as a tyranny. Doug on his 2,000-mile run to Darwin has friends all along the road. He carries $500 to buy things for people along the track, and charges only a few cents for the orders he can fill — anything from beer to seedlings to young trees to car parts.

We saw him again, overtaking him (not easily) in amongst the baobabs and red rocks of the Kimberleys. We had a few beers by the road and said goodbye, for we were heading for Kalumburu Mission, while he was going on to Darwin. *No worries*, he assured us, *I'll see you on my way back.*

Six days later we came down through the hills on to the causeway over the Great Victoria river. Down towards us from the other side came a white Mercedes semi-trailer. *Doug!* We waved. He honked. On the other side of the Victoria I turned the car and we went back. A hotel was providentially ready for us on the western bank. One of Doug's tyres had blown, and he had been waiting to change the wheel until he could have a few beers to get his strength up. He had a nice young passenger, Ken, who had been on his way from Darwin to Perth when his car broke down near Hall's Creek. So he got a lift with Doug to Perth via Darwin. What did an extra thousand miles matter? Good luck, Doug, wherever you are now!

From Wyndham we flew to Kalumburu, the Spanish Benedictine Mission in the furthest North-West, on the King Edward river. After the weird flat whorls of dried mud near Wyndham, and the endless empty rocky hills cut with black rivers, we flew into a smoky haze that almost obscured the ground. The pilot said that about this time of year the Aborigines and the station managers burned off the dry growth over hundreds of square miles to make ready for the wet and the young green growth that would follow. Eventually the smoke fog cleared, and suddenly there below were the neat houses and the gardens and the stone Mission building (rebuilt after being bombed by the Japanese) of Kalumburu. The Mission was founded by Bishop Torres in 1908, and is now under the direction of Father Seraphim Sanz, who has been there since 1939, with Father Eugene Perez and Father Patrick Turner assisting. There are also four Spanish Sisters. The Benedictines keep a daily diary, and Father Perez has written an excellent history of the Mission.

We talked philosophy, anthropology and history with Father Perez, a Spaniard from Burgos who studied art in Melbourne in the late 1940's. He pointed to a sentence in Mircea Eliade's *Australian Religions*: *The Australians have only mythological knowledge, no philosophy*. I suggested that we modern Australians had neither mythological knowledge nor philosophy.

To begin to understand the Aborigines, said Father Perez, *you must agree with Lucien Levy-Bruhl that they have* une mentalité prélogique. *The advantage of this prelogical mentality*, he went on, *is that in its world of contradictions, myths, dreams and reality have the same value, and are interchangeable. There is an affinity with Zen, because Zen cannot be approached intellectually*. He looked on his shelves for a book by W.E.H Stanner, to illustrate his argument with the myths of Kunmanggur and Mutjingga. We talked for hours.

In 1975, in accordance with Government policy, the Fathers were prepared to hand over the Mission, its gardens and pastoral concerns to the Aborigines for them to run themselves. The Aborigines rejected this plan; they wanted the Fathers to stay. It is just as well, as the whole well-run enterprise would collapse without their firm and practical direction. Even now, the local tribes of Aborigines are dying out, with their population only about 200, and would undoubtedly have become extinct without the Mission's support.

The Spaniards, with their love and deep knowledge of the Aborigines, are essentially practical and straightforward men. They are well aware that *the prelogical mentality* does not accord with the white man's order and efficiency, which of course the Aborigines are only too happy to live with, for its material benefits. Spiritual benefits are more mysterious.

We were standing outside the old stone building when some full-blooded Aborigines came along, with their slow, ruminative walk. A handsome middle-aged woman stopped, laughing, to talk to Father Sanz. She embraced him and he slapped her on the back and they spoke in her language. At the gate nearby, in the middle of the road, a stud Brahman bull with three children on his back stared at us. We walked with Father Sanz to the open, circular tanks in the garden. They were full of young crocodiles.

Canberra had had the bright idea of a crocodile farm run by the Aborigines. The big salt-water crocodiles and the little freshwater Johnstone crocodiles are very plentiful in the area; before restrictions on shooting, 4,000 of them were slaughtered in one year. Canberra sent 'an expert' to Kalumburu (*A very nice man*, said Father Sanz). But he turned out to be a linguist, who knew nothing about crocodiles. He finally produced three little crocs, but Father Sanz saw that they were Johnstone crocodiles, and pointed out their characteristic long narrow jaw. *Oh no*, said the expert, *that's only because they're young, they'll get broader when they're older.*

Another expert took the first one's place. *He was also a* very nice man, and *a zoologist, and when he arrived he said, 'I know nothing about crocodiles, but I'm happy to learn.'* So Father Sanz himself went out and collected lots of eggs, and hatched them in the room alongside the

Country town . . . West.

Country town . . . East.

dining hall, and now there are crocodiles in the pools. But the Aborigines don't want anything to do with the project, and the expert has long since gone home. Meanwhile the crocodiles are getting bigger and bigger. It was all a typical 'Northern development scheme for the benefit of the Aborigines'.

Father Perez took us around the huge garden that feeds everyone on the Mission. There was every sort of fruit and vegetable, flanked by great dark green trees dangling with thousands of fat mangoes. But the garden is, in miniature, the story of agriculture in the North. The monks began with virgin soil. Unlike the original Mission on the coast, the present site has an unlimited water supply from the King Edward river, but the soil needs heavy applications of phosphate and other fertilizers. The keeper of the Mission diary wrote on 18 August 1953, *This is the land of plenty, and we have reason to be grateful for such blessings . . . Father Rosendo did the planting, King Edward does the watering, and God gives the increase.*

The improvidence of the Aborigines worries the Fathers. One day Brother John the gardener found a group of boys hurling half-ripe pineapples at each other. The same boys had broken a duck's leg and wing by throwing green lemons at it. Father Sanz told us that each house – and they were proper, comfortable houses, not the dog kennels on so many Aboriginal settlements – had been provided with grapefruit, orange and lemon trees, a mango, tomatoes and other vegetables. The Aborigines let the trees die and the children threw green tomatoes at each other. There were a couple of flourishing, cherished gardens, but if the householders go away for a day the children rush in and tear up the plants.

Those children, allowed to throw green tomatoes at each other, are like the old hymn, *All things bright and beautiful.* Aboriginal children, in their physique, their colouring and their vivacity, must be as beautiful as any children on earth. Even in school they were like the dark side of quicksilver, their eyes darting everywhere. When one of them showed my wife a painting he was doing (which was full of talent), she said *Lovely.* Quickly one of the girls mimicked her perfectly and in a second the whole class was saying *Lovely* and giggling.

But always when you talk to Aboriginal children you go away sad. There they are, beautiful, intelligent, spirited, happy to learn, brilliantly talented in art, dance and mime. And what happens to them? The old paternalistic, inhuman idea was to take them away from their parents to educate them and 'give them a chance'. For the full horror of that experience, one should read Xavier Herbert's *Poor Fellow My Country*, a work of tragic (and comic) genius. Xavier Herbert is one of the few articulate Australians who share some of the Aborigines' profound and mystical love of Australia, and his harshest ferocities are reserved for those who betray this love.

In the evening at Kalumburu we went over to watch an old movie. Obviously, the Aborigines had all seen it before, and they mimicked the dialogue and laughed word perfect, five seconds before the soundtrack. The Sisters sat in a silent row, not missing a word of the two dialogues. The Aborigine managing the projector was serious and efficient; it had been his job for years.

In the North, time and again, you have a strange feeling of suspended animation. There it all is, alive and working, but what is going to happen? The crocodile farm was a perfect symbol, as, on a giant scale, is the Ord river scheme a couple of hundred miles away.

As a tourist attraction it is awe-inspiring. The dam has created in Lake Argyle an incredible blue distance in the red mountains, an inland sea, and miles away at Kununurra the irrigated farms stretch green for miles over the pale, dry landscape. As a practical project most people think it has been a disaster. The insects ate all the cotton, the birds are eating the rice. Once again, for a tourist the birds are a marvellous attraction; I have never seen so many brolgas and jabiru, gravely stooping over the delicious titbits provided by generous man. Swarms of magpie geese flew past, and every other waterbird in the North has been a beneficiary of the Ord.

The Ord river scheme is a sitting shot for hostile journalists and cynics from the South. But Jim, an ex-CSIRO farmer, who took us around his soya, sorghum and rice, and drove us over to see the sugar, is fiercely confident. True, anything will grow there, and since cotton has been abandoned the insect, if not the bird, problems are under control. Even so, all the Ord seems to need is a deep-sea port, a cessation of interstate rivalries (especially among the sugar growers in Queensland) and a stable international market; maybe one possibility and two impossibilities. The Ord, like so much in the North-West, such as the power waiting to be generated by the 35-foot tides, has an immense potential that needs a display of national confidence for it to be realized. But neither politicians nor people in the South have any confidence in the North.

In a suburban Darwin that has had all its individuality blown away in cyclone Tracy, we talked to an old friend, Slim Bauer, who was in charge of the North Australia Research Unit of the Australian National University. He had recently organized a seminar on *Cropping in North Australia: Anatomy of Success and Failure*.

The experts gathered together, and in this case they were genuine experts, but they did not have any easy comfort to offer. There is no doubt that the North could support a large population, as long as they were African- or Asian-style subsistence farmers, but their standard of living would clash disastrously with the rest of Australia. The 30,000 Aborigines in the North, many of whom used to be scattered in family units round the stations, have now mostly gravitated to towns and settlements. On the whole, they have not been interested in agriculture, but this is not necessarily so, as witness the success of the Djudja Aboriginal Group producing broome millet at Kununurra. According to Dr. Millington, from the West Australian office of regional administration in Perth, this *could be developed into a highly productive unit supplying a large proportion of the millet now imported into Australia*. Another group of Aborigines has been organized to pick up the best of the mangoes that used to fall and rot in the 500 trees in Broome and pack them for shipment to Perth.

Dr. Millington is full of practical suggestions for the development of the North, which would also rescue the Aborigines from their disheartening and destructive plight. But as he and Slim Bauer and many others point out, the North must first be considered a part of Australia, and money must be found. The unpleasant paradox remains, clear to see for anyone who travels around the North, that affluent Australia, happily playing at being a 'developed' country, is in fact a chronically under-developed country. Australia gives about $400 million in foreign aid a year; maybe it would be better for Australia if at least half of that was spent instead on developing and populating the North, and rehabilitating our internal refugees, the Aborigines.

In Darwin stubbies are big bottles — and dangerous goods.

Instant luck?

Confidence

Every nation has its myths, both sustaining and destructive. But probably no nation has more internal critics than Australia, attacking or perverting myths that sustain, and gleefully hailing myths that destroy.

A healthy, cheerful scepticism is characteristically Australian, and it should preserve Australians from the tyrannies of left or right. Unfortunately, Australians are also chronically under-confident in their country and in themselves. When the knocker comes along, especially when he is dealing with myths, Australians believe him.

The sustaining myths are that Australians are the greatest democrats in the world; that they are good mates, good fighters, good drinkers, that they are bronzed and fit and love the beaches and sport, and that the typical Australian is like Banjo Paterson's station-hand:

I'm travellin' down the Castlereagh, and I'm a station hand,
I'm handy with the ropin'-pole, I'm handy with the brand,
And I can ride a rowdy colt, or swing the axe all day.

The true modern image of this, unfortunately, is the man in a Marlboro cigarette advertisement.

The destructive myths are that Australians are sexists (if men, of course), racists, materialists, nationalists, militarists, philistines, narcissists, suckers for advertising, complacently ignorant, violent Ockers, drunkards, gamblers and all fat and out of condition. A visitor like Arthur Koestler comes for a short time entirely spent amongst these destructive myths, and goes away saying Australians have *a fear of the open spaces of the mind.*

In fact, all these destructive myths proliferate in every Western country, and most of them exist undercover in all the other countries in the world. Who could be more sexist than the South American male, more materialistic than a Frenchman, more philistine than an Englishman, more prone to believing advertising than a North American and so on? And even then, these generalizations are simply not true of any country. I always remember the remark of Sir William Emrys Williams, former Secretary General of the Arts Council of Great Britain: *Your average steelworker, just like your average stockbroker, will always be a philistine.* But breaking that down again, there is no such thing as the average steelworker or the average stockbroker.

The only way to test a myth is by individual reality, in effect lining up those who bear it out and those who disprove it. Sometimes there is a draw between the opposing teams, sometimes a clean win or defeat.

It must be admitted that in every area of the relationship between the sexes, Australians do not emerge with much glory. Although the incidence of overt homosexuality was relatively low, the old ideal of Australian mateship was essentially based on freedom from women. An old bushman once said to a friend of mine that Western Australia was all right *till the women and the rabbits moved in.*

I remember at Anlaby some years ago, when two officials of the Merino Stud Breeders' Association came with some documents to be signed, and a witness was required. My brother went down from the woolshed to the house and came back with a Swiss-Australian girl who was staying with us. *No,* said one of the officials, *we want a proper witness, not a woman.*

Racecourses in Australia still have separate enclosures for men and women. The list could be extended painfully and almost indefinitely.

I also remember a station manager, a man who had known my wife for many years, telling her she was not like a woman, and meaning it as a compliment.

The other half of this sad truth is that Australian women, after being treated for so long as second-class citizens, bring their own troubles down on themselves. One night, after a performance in Canberra of David Williamson's hilarious play *Don's Party*, a perfectly intelligent woman said to me, *Of course, it was really a man's evening, only the men were laughing.* I could hardly tell her that the very attractive woman sitting next to me had been falling out of her seat with laughter. Another woman said *Don's Party* was *a terrible comment on society.* An Adelaide woman, apropos of a recent revival of Ray Lawler's classic, *The Summer of the Seventeenth Doll*, made the same remark I had heard at the opening night in Adelaide 23 years ago: *It'll give a dreadful impression of Australia overseas.* They would be shocked to know that those are exactly the sentiments uttered by the hard-line party members in the Moscow Union of Writers about any work of literature presenting the truth about their own country.

Yet the attitudes of the sexes towards each other conform to one of my main themes throughout this book; there have been enormous changes within the last 25 years. These years, even more than the 1890's, have been the great watershed in Australian history, after which nothing will be the same again. A potent influence on sexual relations has been the integration into the population of millions of Europeans. Such changes are more apparent to a beautiful woman than to a man. One such told me that in her opinion the strongarm Australian male approach had had its muscles exposed as cardboard by the European Australian, who did not know that *a ladies' man* was a term of abuse. *How about the English?* I asked. She laughed. *They are the only men who can be both cold and lecherous at the same time.*

She was talking, of course, of the upper-class British. Most Australians, fortunately, have never been exposed either to upper-class Englishmen or English women at their worst. The attitudes of the latter to the colonies have had to be experienced and remembered to be believed. Costly casuals, a friend of ours used to call them.

On one occasion some friends of ours in Melbourne asked us to entertain a visiting English businessman and his wife. The man had engagements, so my wife, despite her private distaste for ladies' lunches, organized one for the visiting Lady. I brought home three beautiful fresh crayfish for them. The Lady then rang to say she couldn't come to lunch on Friday. Her husband was meeting the Premier at 6.15 that day and perhaps she'd better be there, in which case she'd need a good sleep in the early afternoon. *But I'll pop up in the car at 11 for half an hour and see you.* Sure *you haven't been to any trouble? Oh I'm sure you* have.

This episode occurred in the early 1960's, but I do not think it could occur today, not because that type of English upper-class lady does not still exist, but because they would be aware that it is

Just sheilas. Queensland Gold Coast.

Just dial. Sydney.

no longer prudent to patronize Australians. Their husbands would have told them. And of course Britain itself is no longer a centre of power and wealth. (I remember the catalogue Aspreys in Bond Street used to send my mother, with items like *six mother of pearl caviare spreaders*.)

And Australian attitudes have changed. We are learning to laugh at ourselves, not in the back-slapping way of *They're a Weird Mob*, but in Barry Humphries' deadly revelations of our prejudices. Typically, Barry Humphries still from time to time is attacked for *creating a bad image of Australia abroad*. During a recent season in London, Humphries was visited backstage by a young English couple. They told him that they had wanted to emigrate to Australia, until they visited Australia House and talked to officials and read the dreadful official propaganda for Australia. Now, having listened to Dame Edna Everage, Sandy Stone and Les Paterson for an evening, they had decided to emigrate to Australia after all because *Australia must be a good country if Australians can laugh at themselves like that*.

Dame Edna Everage may, alas, be typical of all that is worst in the Australian matron in her 40's. But Barry Humphries, genius though he is, cannot portray a woman in her 20's, and neither Edna's vile prejudices, nor Norm's ineffectual relationship with her, are nearly as valid for the younger women.

I like to think, without sentimentality, of the woman going off to work as a deckhand and part-owner on her husband's prawn trawler as a typical Australian female of the late 1970's. Equally typical is someone like Kate Fitzpatrick, perhaps Australia's most brilliant younger actress. What could be more in the authentic Australian idiom than her recalling her early Christmases in Adelaide: *December was always so hot that hundreds of people slept on the sand and on the water's edge. We were at the beach before the sun rose every morning and ate Christmas lunch sitting on the sand: turkey, ham, watermelon, ice cream and plum pudding. Christmas evening was always spent at my grandmother's with all the family; never less than 30 people covering four generations.*

This sort of access to, and confidence in, a common idiom is what fortifies a nation, or a family, that institution so beleaguered in the modern world. The British have no common idiom, for they are split even now into classes. But all Australians speak the same idiom, albeit with slight variations of accent, so that a foreigner can hardly tell the difference between a Queenslander and South Australian. It is not a question of slang, though Australian colloquialisms are gloriously rich and are apt to be used happily by Australians at all levels of education or income. It is an attitude of mind; no one in Australia is entitled to come the raw prawn on anyone else.

The sense of being Australian has been expressed orally and felt instinctively for more than 100 years, but it can only be consolidated, as in art, literature or film, by the conjunction of two processes, a declaration of independence and a sense of community. In this, life follows art, because these are the two essential processes of all art, transcending naturalism by giving universal humanity a local habitation.

For years Australia, like any other colonial country, has had to battle against those who think that imitation, whether slavish or unconscious, is better than originality. Australia has been particularly unfortunate, as it has had to shake off, or rather absorb what is best of, both the British and American influences.

The myth of being 'British' has worked cruelly on Australians, especially in hypnotizing her young men to rush into wars, from that absurd business in the Sudan, and the Boer War, when Australian bushmen were fighting their own kind, to the two World Wars. It is extraordinary that the holocaust of Gallipoli, often thought to have done more to make Australia a nation than Federation had done 14 years earlier, has never prompted more Australians to question the rights or wrongs of being there. Had those questions been asked, there might have been claims in Australia to regard Winston Churchill, the architect of Gallipoli, as a war criminal. Yet when the Churchill Fund was established after his death, the City of Adelaide subscribed more than Birmingham, Nottingham and Liverpool combined.

Fortunately the Anzac image has survived a period of knocking after what may have been a period of excessive idolatry. A nation could not want for finer heroes; there is a wonderful lyrical expression of that heroic quality in Sidney Nolan's series of paintings in the National War Museum. But with that heroism went a stoic acceptance of a fate more subtle than death from a Turkish bullet. It was the national acceptance of obedience when Britain called, to be followed, 50 years later in Vietnam, by a willingness to rush in even when America had not officially called at all.

I remember a conversation I had with a Melbourne man at a very Establishment party at the time of the Vietnam war. He began by asking me why I was a Communist. This accusation was based on the fact that I had recently been to the Soviet Union and had written various articles about it. He then asked me, *What three things would you do first if you were a Prime Minister with real power?* I asked him if he wanted a serious answer. He assured me he did. So I said, *I would stop the Vietnam war. I would recognize Communist China. I would try to do something about Australian racism, both inside the country in relation to the Aborigines, and outside in relation to Asia in particular.* To which he took another gin and replied, *None of these three things has anything to do with Australia. You and I were brought up to do as we were told. We went to World War II because the Government told us to. That's all the Vietnam war consists of.*

The attitude to Britain was that of a family tie, taken for granted by Britain, unquestioned by Australia. This mental and spiritual deference of a proud people has been very confusing for younger generations of Australians. It was further confused by the adoption of the USA as protector during World War II, and after Australia sent troops to Vietnam it took some time before a reaction gathered strength. Prime Minister Harold Holt's *All the way with LBJ* was only another version of Andrew Fisher's pledge on the outbreak of World War I of *Our last man and shilling.* As an English journalist resident in Australia in 1914 patronizingly put it: *The declaration of war was not taken quite so calmly by the Australian people as by the people of the United Kingdom. The Australians, as a youthful community, naturally exercise less restraint in a time of Imperial stress than the experienced veterans of the Mother Country.*

A youthful community . . . Imperial stress. One has only to read some of the heartrending letters or diaries of World War I Anzacs to

Limited entertainment . . . Melbourne.

Entertainment unlimited . . . Adelaide.

realize how like schoolboys the youth of Australia volunteered for the great game of Empire. *The bravest thing God ever made*, a British officer wrote of the Australian soldier.

But bravery in what? In fighting another country's wars. In her noble tribute to that bravery, based on soldiers' letters and diaries, Patsy Adam-Smith illustrates the sad theme that Australia did not become an Australian nation at Federation in 1901; she became a British nation. There is an order from the Minister of Education in Victoria in the *Education Gazette and Teacher's Aid* of 29 October, 1901, quoted by Adam-Smith, that in order to increase patriotism, *Lessons inculcating patriotism be given, songs of a national character be sung, and the ceremony of saluting the flag be performed.* The Minister suggested the following programme:

Oral lesson: Life of King Edward VII
Patriotic song
Oral lesson: The Union Jack
Saluting the flag
Patriotic song
Oral lesson: The British Empire
Patriotic verses by the children
The National Anthem

Apart from the fact that the mind boggles at children really being taught about the life of King Edward VII, the reality of the Minister's programme is British, not Australian. For him, 'patriotic' meant 'British'. Of course, until recently Australians were called British on their passports, not Australian. As of 1901 there was no national flag. A competition was called, and five different designs were exhibited in September, 1901. Not until 1903 did the King approve a national flag, which of course incorporated the Union Jack.

Last in the Education Minister's programme for the school children, the National Anthem was, of course, *God Save the King*. Seventy-nine years later Australia still has neither a true national flag nor anthem. When the first contingent of the Australian Expeditionary Force left here in October, 1914, they were serenaded by an obnoxious song, of which the chorus ran

For Britain! Good old Britain!
Where our fathers first drew breath,
We'll fight like true Australians,
Facing danger, wound or death.
With Britain's other gallant sons
We're going hand in hand;
Our War-cry 'Good old Britain' boys
Our own dear Motherland.

One of the most important of the accepted myths is that Australia was welded as a nation in the fire of Gallipoli, and that Anzac Day, 25 April, is the solemnizing of the experience. This is only true in the sense of forging a community, a bond between people, a national admiration of bravery, and a day of mourning for so many dead.

But Australia was not a nation, she was *For Britain! Good old Britain!* The truth about Gallipoli and France only rarely emerged, as in an Australian officer's uncensored letter to his sister: *The A.E.F. are being used as nothing else than gun fodder.*

Australians were already distinctively Australian, in their idiom and in their attitude to their land, by the middle of the 19th century. But the true moulding of Australia as a nation, which has still not been completed, did not begin at Gallipoli, but in the slow discovery that Britain, if the occasion demanded, would betray and abandon Australia. Australians began to learn this unsingable truth in the great depression of the 1930's, when the Bank of England dictated Australia's economy, and after the fall of Singapore in 1942. If Winston Churchill deserves the obloquy of the Australians for sending the Anzacs to Gallipoli, how much more so does he deserve it for trying to stop John Curtin, the Australian Prime Minister, from bringing the Australian troops back from the Middle East to defend Australia from the Japanese.

Australians learned the final economic truth about their relations with 'the Mother Country' when Britain entered the Common Market. The economic ties were broken, as were the sentimental ones, when Australian visitors to Britain found they had to enter through the gate marked 'Aliens'.

But the emergence of the true nature of British-Australian relationships should mean a strengthening and maturing of ties between the two countries. The growing number of those who want an Australian Republic do not want Australia to sever her links with Britain; there are plenty of Republics in the Commonwealth already. Unfortunately there is more awareness in Australia of British-Australian realities than there is in Britain, where most people are either not aware of Australia at all or think of Australians as rather faded cricketers or as a mob of Bazza Mackenzies. Bazza was a case of a satirical creation, the Oz in London, which got away from its creator, Barry Humphries, and became a reality among Australians, who tried to live down to this image of them.

Fortunately, at this crucial period in Australian history, when the need has become acute for Australians to have a clear vision of themselves speaking their own idiom, the long-moribund Australian film industry has burst into renewed life. After producing some of the first features in the world, the Australians suffered the colonial fate of having the local work extinguished by imported films from the UK and the USA. Recently directors like Peter Weir, Fred Schepisi and Bruce Beresford, and producers like the McElroy brothers and Joan Long have made films which have successfully gone around the world. These films have exported Australia's vision of itself. Above all, they have nourished that drought-stricken plant, Australian self-confidence.

To see your own people and hear your own idiom on the screen is essential for any people being constantly bombarded with foreign material. The imbalance has been, and is, even worse on television than the cinema. On a recent, and typical Saturday night, there were 24 TV programmes, 11 of which were repeats. The 24 consisted of six US movies, eight US serials, five British movies and serials, one Australian serial, one Australian coverage of a local pageant, two Australian news programmes and one goodnight programme.

Under this barrage of brainwashing, the fact that ordinary Australians still manage to be unmistakably Australian must reveal a deep and powerful national identity, however under-

The Palais.

The Palace.

confident people are in their recognition of this identity.

Unfortunately the very people who should help Australian self-confidence, both at home and abroad, often betray it. A Patrick White or a Barry Humphries may mercilessly expose our shortcomings; that is good for us. Exposure to such light helps kill the germs. But the knockers are still busy in Australia; and there is still a lamentable lack of sophistication in the handling of our interests abroad. There was an awful example recently in a campaign to sell Australian wine overseas. Anyone with a genuine knowledge of wine would be happy to tell you that Australian wines are some of the best in the world. But instead of a serious and dignified approach to people who do not know this, an exporter recently sent 1,000 bottles of Hunter reds to France under the label 'Kanga Rouge'. It was the sort of programme Bazza Mackenzie would have sponsored.

As for the diplomats, nothing has changed with them in the last 20 years. In Kim Bonython's autobiography he recalls the difficulties of organizing the showing of the great Mertz collection of modern Australian art in the USA. An exhibition finally opened at the Corcoran Gallery in Washington, DC, in March, 1967. Bonython comments: *The former US Ambassador to Australia, Ed Clark, was far more enthusiastic about the whole project, I am rather ashamed to say, than our own Embassy staff.* Anybody who remembers Ed Clark will know what a deadly comment this is.

It is not the Australian people who are basically at fault. Rather, they tend to accept the lack of confidence demonstrated by many of those who claim to speak for Australia. Whatever its political failings, the great achievement of the Whitlam years was a surge of pride in things Australian that came down to the country from the top. And Mr. Fraser is conscious of this; he gives national broadcasts urging people not to knock Australia. But at the top the old colonial attitudes persist and the subtle denigration of Australian talent and quality goes on, hinting that the homegrown cannot be any good.

For example, it was only very recently that Qantas, 'Australia's National Airline', first employed an Australian advertising agency instead of an American one.

The Adelaide telephone directory for 1978-79 depicted an early autumn scene in the gardens of a house in the Adelaide hills. With maple leaves littering the grass (behind the legend 'Too lovely to Litter'), it reminds me of nothing so much as Roundhay Park in Leeds in Yorkshire. Not an Australian flower or tree is visible. By a hidden irony, that same garden, before it was planted with European trees 45 years ago, contained one of the finest collections of native plants in Australia, all of which were removed to make way for the exotics.

Most Australians are too easy-going to notice such things, but of course nonchalance invites manipulation. J.D. Pringle, some years ago in a book on Australia, shrewdly observed: *The easy-going nature of the Australian, which D.H. Lawrence recognised, has not protected him from the encroachment of modern bureaucracy, and has merely allowed bureaucrats to impose on him more easily.*

There is a paradox here. D.H. Lawrence also noticed the average Australian's unconcern and irreverence for authority. Every Australian must cherish memories of this irreverence. I remember once going to the beautiful old Theatre Royal in Adelaide, now alas pulled down to make room for a parking station. We were sitting in the stalls, right under the balcony of the Dress Circle. Suddenly there was a hush, and everyone stood up. A very Australian voice behind us said, *What the bloody hell's going on? It's the Governor coming in,* said another. *He's sitting right above us. Well,* said the spectator, sitting down, *he'd better not drop his bloody peanut shells on me.*

In 1958 the Queen Mother visited Adelaide, and society ladies and gentlemen were in paroxysms of anxiety over invitations and opportunities to shake the royal hand. Vast sums were spent on new dresses and hats. The social comedy was delicious. On the day of the 'royal progress' through the city, crowds lined the streets and there was a stand for VIPs in front of the Town Hall. At the last moment a City Council garbage truck drove between the crowds massed along King William Street, manned by three hairy-legged blokes in shorts, one of them bending his wrist slowly in a regal acknowledgement to the crowd. Twenty years later, one can imagine the same scene from the garbage truck, but not from the populace. Royalty could not draw crowds like that nowadays. It no longer rhymes with loyalty, despite the lip service paid to the crown by certain sections of the media.

Deep down there still is a profound respect for authority, although it may not be quite as deep as it was. It seems amazing now that only 20 years ago Australians were putting up with licensing laws that shut the pubs at six and took wine glasses off the dinner table at eight. Even today, in Queensland the citizens are still not allowed to read *Playboy*, let alone march in the streets without a special permit.

It is those in authority in Australia who have the most respect for authority. This respect used to take the form of colonial attitudes, which still exist, to a certain extent. Nowadays it is manifested mostly in lack of confidence. Overseas businessmen visiting Australia have been astonished at the meekness in the young Australian executives. An English merchant banker told me he was taken to lunch at a club by a group of Melbourne business-men. *And it was more conservative than anything I could have believed possible.*

A profound conservatism underlies the easy-going Australian manner. Fortunately it is balanced by a sardonic humour and a dislike of any pomposity or affectation. Thus, although Australian political life swings more often to a conservative status quo than a radical experimentation, it is unlikely that a dictator would ever establish himself in Australia. There have also been enough free spirits to wake up their fellow Australians when liberties were threatened. A century ago, the melancholy, mellifluous Henry Kendall sharply denounced Henry Parkes' attempt to introduce a Bill to gag the Press, and reviled all those

Who placed your freedom in the reach of sharks,
And fell from Pericles to – Henry Parkes!

The poet Les Murray, a conservative country man with some radical but no trendy ideas, has the true Australian blend of scepticism and deep, unannounced belief. He is proof against the world of advertising and the good news of instant foods. Reading a

Bondi Beach.

Surfers' Paradise.

poem of his, *Immigrant Voyage*, about his wife's coming to Australia as a migrant from Europe, I came upon the lines

and further ahead
in the years of the Coffee Revolution
and the Smallgoods Renaissance.

They brought back to me a journey, in 1951, around northern Victorian country towns, giving lectures for the Commonwealth Literary Fund. We stayed in fine freezing old 1890's pubs, high and white with pots along the façade, and cast-iron lace around the verandahs. Inside one classic example were bronze statuettes of William Shakespeare and John Milton, a head of Beethoven, faded old needlework panels with threaded names, Venezia, Napoli, Roma. At the head of the stairs was a huge alabaster urn, in front of a window with the blind half-down and two thick red curtains. Outside my room was a marble girl in a nightie, holding her arms out and looking rather foolish because someone had broken both her hands off.

In the dead silence of the dining room, so different from the roar of the bar, a dozen men were eating. It was arctic cold and the fireplace looked as if it had been last lit for opening night in 1892. For dinner there was soup, roast mutton, and a choice of steamed pudding or apricot tart, both stone cold. A nice Italian at our table had been eating there for three years. Three years! It was unimaginable. He said, *I suppose you never had cold steamed pudding before? No*, said the young man who was driving me from town to town and introducing my lectures. *We have. This is the same one we have been eating for three months.*

At breakfast a tall, bony waitress brusquely offered us tea or coffee. My companion told me that the last time he had been waited on by her he was looking after a Viennese opera singer, who was giving lectures and recitals. This lady, on being offered coffee, had said to the waitress, *Is it real or essence?*

Sorry dear, don't follow yer.

I mean, is it made with grounds, is it Brazil, Kilimanjaro, light roast, dark roast, or does it come out of a bottle?

Neither, dear, it come out of a 44-gallon drum.

That had its cold reality, which was not inferior to the anxious sophistication of *the years of the Coffee Revolution and the Smallgoods Renaissance.* Australians have now discovered there is nothing wrong with sticking to drinking tea, if you like it better than coffee.

The Australian mixture of conservatism and scepticism has got the country through a new crisis of confidence caused by what may later be called The Sophisticated '70's. The impact of the European migration had been accepted, the arts were flourishing, and a new breed of pseudosophisticates were attempting to tyrannize Australians. Those French menus in Tom Price or Kununurra were a spin-off. The latest and most horrendous of Barry Humphries' creations, Sir Leslie Paterson, is the Cultural Attaché of an Australia *second to none in terms of macramé, pomes, opera, modesty, TV, and Aboriginal artifacts,* and the promoter of his own book *arguably a celebration of one man's on-going, open-ended, down-market, across-the-board, grass-roots Australian situation, hopefully.*

Australia can live with Humphries, and with those who create their order from its chaos – White, Xavier Herbert, Judith Wright – however fierce their criticisms. But we can do without those who cannot forgive Australia for not being something else. All the Anglophiles, for whom Wagga Wagga will never look like Cirencester, a gum tree never redden in autumn like a maple, for whom 'beaut' will never sound as cultivated as 'absolutely marvellous'. All those academics, for whom the Romans never left a ruin in Alice Springs, for whom Adam Lindsay Gordon was not Lord Byron, for whom the Adelaide *Advertiser* is not the London *Times*. All the knockers, for whom the Paris end of Collins Street is not the Champs Elysées, for whom Grange Hermitage is not Château Lafite. All those moralists, for whom John Olsen's *You Beaut Country* is the Slough of Despond. All those who will never forgive Australians for being Australian, nor Australian civilization for being, in terms of the white man, so young. Yet most Australians, whether living in Woolloomooloo or Sarsaparilla or Upotipotpon, have an odd abiding confidence that their own lives and those of their neighbours are of importance. As the children grow into expected roles or into scientists or opera singers they never imagine that they are living in an Australia where *The river of her immense stupidity/Floods her monotonous tribes from Cairns to Perth*. And A.D. Hope himself, who wrote those lines many years ago, now drives through the countryside in his old Valiant station-wagon savouring the names, and hears a different music as

> *a latter-day Habbakuk*
> *Rises in me to preach comic sermons of doom,*
> *Crying: 'Woe unto Tocumwal, Teddywaddy, Tooleybuk!'*
> *And: 'Wicked Wallumburrowang your hour has come!'*

For he has found the place where the prophet may be at rest, although not be silenced, and when the Last Judgement unleashes the final bush fire in Australia

> *One place shall sing and flourish in the fire:*
> *It is Sweet Water Creek at Mullangandra*
> *And there at the Last Day I shall retire.*

For those who go out from the cities, Australia can still run with sweet water and work miracles of healing, drought-stricken though it is. For those who stay in the cities, and open the doors, there are books, paintings, theatres, dance, chamber music and choirs as well as football and the races. Despite unemployment, economic problems and the unresolved dilemma of the Aborigines, no other country in the world has such an uninhibited full life for most of the population as Australia.

I was recently listening on the radio to a French girl who had ridden a motor cycle, on her own, around Australia. *I felt so free,* she said. Exactly. Australia must be the freest country on earth, despite the multitude of petty rules and regulations. Not only political freedom, but the freedom of space and distance, and the freedom between people who do not want to interfere with each other's pleasures.

The snags below the quiet, easy-running, brown surface are there, of course, but they are not as deep as the river. Australians can be thankful for many good things. Australia has no terrorists, no civil wars; you are not liable to receive an explosive parcel through the post or be bombed in a restaurant. Australia has no tyrants, no assassinations, no race riots, no violent extremes of rich and poor. Her cities are almost free of slums and ghettos; there are no city blocks of misery and desolation. Her blessings ought to be counted. What has to be done is plenty, but there is no harm in thinking of what is already growing in the most arid continent on earth.

Home made, Queensland.